THE BOOK OF BOOK OF MONEY LISTS

THE BOOK OF MONEY LISTS

Philip Dunn

Illustrated by Peregrine

ARROW BOOKS

Arrow Books Limited
17–21 Conway Street, London W1P 6JD

An imprint of the Hutchinson Publishing Group

London Melbourne Sydney Auckland
Johannesburg and agencies throughout
the world

First published 1985
© Philip Dunn 1985
Illustrations © Peregrine 1985

Set in Linotron Baskerville by
Input Typesetting Ltd, London

Printed and bound in Great Britain by
Anchor Brendon Limited, Tiptree, Essex

ISBN 0 09 940910 0

*This book is dedicated to
my son and daughter, Benjamin and Lily –
with love*

Contents

Section Three   Money Words

Section Four   Bad Money

Section Five   Pay Day

Introduction

If an alien power from another world came to Earth and demanded to know the value of this planet, bringing out a large chequebook and drawing a writing instrument into one of his six hands, how much would we assess the world we live in to be worth? A trillion? A billion trillion? How would we express this balance sheet? In what currency?

Some world currencies are not worth the paper they are printed on, such as the Hungarian 10 million billion pengo note, widely used in 1946 when prices in Budapest went up ten times in a day. I'm sure that our alien visitor would not be duped by such an expression of value. Most values on an international scale are expressed in dollars – US dollars. But where would the value of the world come from? Gold, diamonds, national product, property, cash? How willing would we be to sell up and start over? Somebody would have to sit down and make a list of everything worth anything all over the planet.

The Book of Money Lists is a starting point for such a task, and now that it is complete, if the aliens come, we can at least bargain without setting out from scratch.

It is, of course, virtually impossible to assess the exact value of the world in financial terms. However, there are many aspects of world finance where we can make a very clear list. Of all the commodities, money is the one of which people keep most precise records, particularly in the past hundred years.

From the very beginning, when the concept of exchanging metal coins for goods was devised, the power to acquire has been largely associated with the use of money. The world is now so money oriented that it is hard to conceive of ever again dealing with day to day matters without its presence, in whatever form it develops. Everything within the commercial and political world is totally dependent on large quantities of money. By comparison with an ordinary individual's requirements, the quantities in use within commerce seem like telephone numbers; they have no real meaning to us – there is no way of actually conceiving what a million dollars feels like, unless we have something we can directly compare with it. There is a story of a couple who won half a million dollars on a lottery. They paid in the money to their bank and then a few days later went back and asked the manager to draw the whole lot in cash. The manager respectfully did so, counting out the full amount in one-dollar bills at the clients' request, on to a large table. Once it was all there, a few hours of counting later, the couple said, 'Thank you very much, you can put it all away again now, we just wanted to see how it looked.'

But *The Book of Money Lists* attempts to give comparisons: large with small, small with smaller and poverty with incredible riches. Some of the sums of money mentioned in the book are so staggeringly large that it does not seem likely that there could ever be that much anywhere in such a small planet. Of course, figures are one thing, liquidity is another; and very often the large sums do not exist in fact – only on paper.

But then, nowadays all money exists on paper – all money is paper. Gone are the days when every dollar or pound was backed by gold reserves. Only about one third of the cash in circulation is backed by gold bars and that proportion will probably lessen.

Money is energy, a sophisticated and convenient form of energy which we have devised to help us bring intangible forces within our everyday grasp. The more energy we actually have for money, concentrated on money, the more we make, and the more we make the more we spend (with notable exceptions, like Mrs Green, the notorious miser – see item 4 of '5 very, very rich people'), and so the spiral devalues our fascination for money.

All types of money transaction can be related to one or other of these four devices: work, beggary, crime and usury. Throughout *The Book of Money Lists* the same four systems appear constantly. The richest people have either become rich through working, stealing, borrowing or inheriting their money and the world's poor have gone without because they have not worked, they have failed to steal successfully, borrowed too much (or lent too much) or been given nothing (or given everything). We could call this the four elements of money.

Money can be very serious: we spend it on survival, war, death, birth, sex, chance; all the most basic and emotional things. But it can also be extremely funny: we spend it on entertainment, excess, holidays, love. The things that some people choose to spend it on, others could never understand – how could anyone want to throw away a million dollars on one party, or charter a jumbo jet for one trip across the Atlantic? It's all relative. For the same amount of money in one country or another we can buy vastly different quantities of the same item. In London six bananas cost almost a pound – in India for a pound you could buy 200 bananas.

At the other end of the scale from bananas, the amount of money we spend on entertainment continues to have a dramatic effect on a very small number of people. Some of the richest people in the world are in show business. Marlon Brando is said to have been paid over a million pounds for a few minutes' appearance in *Superman* – that's about £2000 per second. The average working man will be lucky to make that in a couple of months. Bananas, isn't it?

But the business of money is advancing, just as science and all other matters of life are advancing. With the growth in technology the power that money can bring increases. The computer transfer systems operated in the USA will shortly link between all the banks and many retail outlets so that the movement of money will be so fast that payments can be deducted from private accounts within seconds. The credit card becomes more sophisticated each year: American Express will soon instigate a system whereby none of the paperwork of cash collection is needed – payments will be deducted electronically and automatically. We will all, soon, be walking around with computer-linked credit cards which tie directly into our bank accounts and it is estimated that this device alone will gain the banking system over 54 billion dollars in available revenue each year.

But where does all this speed and extra profit leave us? One day perhaps computers will correspond so fast that we'll be paid even before we've done the work – then the whole thing will start to go backwards! The speed at which the use of money increases will either help more people to wealth and comfort or simply line the pockets of those who already have it. That depends not on the money, but on those who handle it.

But in all this, *The Book of Money Lists* is only an innocent bystander – simply giving the information and letting the reader make judgements.

Section One

FUNNY MONEY

If money is a joke to you, then you probably have its measure. But the measure of money is finely balanced – so beware, should the joke be on you.

39

of the most expensive things in the world, and some of the people who could afford them

Everybody loves to know about things they cannot afford. So here is a list of 39 of the most expensive things you couldn't afford to buy and a few of the people who could.

1. A 50-gram or 1.76-ounce tin of First Choice Black Perigord truffles costs £30.

2. The most expensive college in the world is the St Andrews Private Tutorial Centre in Cambridge where in the year 1981–2 the charges were £7648.50 for one student including tuition and accommodation.

3. On 6 April 1982 Jim Priceman, an assistant cashier at Doft and Co. in New York City found an envelope containing negotiable bearer bonds certificates worth $37 million outside a Wall Street office. The certificates could have been cashed by him, freely, but he returned them to their owner. The reward was $250! Expensive honesty.

4. The most expensive jumble sale in the world took place at the Cleveland Convention Center, Ohio, in

October 1981 where 2500 volunteers collected $382,270.

5. The most expensive wedding reception took place at the Croix de Bouquets presidential ranch on 27 May 1980 between Jean-Claude Duvalier and Michelle Bennet and is reported to have cost Haiti's National Treasury something over a million dollars.

6. The most expensive cigarette card is a Honus Wagner American Tobacco Co. card sold in New York in December 1981 for £25,000.

7. The most expensive life assurance policy was sold by Lorenzo Reyes for the Trans America Occidental Life Assurance Co. Inc. on behalf of a Calgary land developer whose life was covered for $44 million.

8. The most expensive clock in the world was bought by the British Museum in July 1982 for £500,000. It was made by Thomas Tompion.

9. The most expensive house is Kenstead Hall in Hampstead with its beautiful beech woods, owned by the late king of Saudi Arabia and put up for sale in August 1982 for £16 million.

10. The most expensive hotel in the world is the Nova Park Élysées in Paris where the royal suite costs £3900 per day. One of the second most expensive is the official New York City Presidential Suite in the Waldorf Astoria which runs at $2000 a day (£1700).

11. The most expensive TV advertising time was during NBC's Superbowl on 24 January 1982 when the rate was $690,000 per minute.

12. The most expensive movie recorded to date was *Star Trek* which set Paramount Studios back to the tune of $46 million prior to its premier in 1979. Just by way of contrast – the movie of *Rescued by Rover* made in 1905 by Cecil Hepworth cost £7 13s 9d!

13.   The most expensive price paid for movie rights was $9,500,000 for *Annie* by Columbia.

14.   The most expensive dog was Indian Joe, a greyhound bought by Alf McLean in Ireland in June 1980 after he won the 50th Greyhound Derby at White City in London. Mr McLean paid £40,000 for the animal.

15.   The most expensive pigeon was purchased by a Japanese fancier. The bird's name was De Witslager and it cost around £25,000.

16.   The most expensive horse was the 1969 All American Futurity winner Easy Jet, which was syndicated for $30 million in fifty shares of $600,000 each share.

17.   The highest-earning golf player is Jack Nicklaus who, up to July 1982, had won $3,972,446.

18.   The most expensive footballer was Bryan Robson for whom Manchester United paid West Bromwich Albion £1,500,000.

19.   The most expensive annual phone bill is that of the Pentagon in Washington DC with 25,000 lines and an annual bill of $8.7 million.

20.   The most expensive spice is *Panax quinquefolius* or wild ginseng which is thought to have aphrodisiac qualities and fetches as much as £23,000 per ounce in Hong Kong.

21.   The most expensive fruit was a pound of strawberries sold in April 1977 in Ireland by John Synnott for £530.

22. The most expensive coin collection was a hoard of 407,000 US silver dollars, sold in a Reno, Nevada auction in 1976 for $7,300,000.

23. The most expensive hospitals in the world are in California where an average daily stay would run up a bill of $615 in 1984.

24. The most expensive sheep was $A79,000 for a merino ram from South Australia at the Adelaide Show on 10 September 1981.

25. The most expensive pig was a Duroc boar named Glacier who was sold for $42,500 in February 1979.

26. The highest price ever paid for a cow was $300,000 for a Holstein-Friesian in Walton, New York, in November 1980.

27. The most expensive bull was Joe's Pride, who fetched $2,500,000 in California in September 1974.

28. The most expensive vase was appraised a four-sided Kang Hsi piece in Phoenix Arizona, valued in 1978 at $60 million.

29. The most expensive wreath was that sent to the funeral of President Kennedy on 25 November 1963 by the civic authority of Paris, handled by Interflora and costing $1200.

30. The most expensive writing paper is sold by Cartier on Fifth Avenue in New York for $100 per sheet and envelope. It is hand-made in Finland and contains a personalized portrait watermark.

31. The most expensive pipe is a Meerschaum pipe with the bowl sculptured into Anthony and Cleopatra, priced at $15,000 in San Diego, California.

32. The highest price paid for a pot lid is £3300 for a patterned 'Spanish Lady' lid sold at Phillips in London in 1982.

33. The most expensive hat in the world was Emperor Napoleon I's, purchased by Moet & Chandon for 165,570 (£14,000) francs in 1970.

34. The highest-priced dress ever sold was exhibited by a Paris fashion house in 1977, called 'The Birth of Venus', designed by Serge Lepage with 500 diamonds, and priced at around £880,000.

35. The most expensive beer can in the world sold in the US for $6000 in April 1981. It was a Rosalie Pilsner.

36. The most expensive place in the world to rent space is Hong Kong, where, according to *World Rental Levels* by Richard Ellis, a square foot of it costs £30.58. New York City follows close with £29.89 per square foot and London third with £28.

37. The most expensive land in the world is also in Hong Kong where in 1981 a corporation purchased land at £3104 per square foot.

38. In October 1971, for the Imperial Iranian 2500th Anniversary gathering at Persepolis, a 5½-hour banquet included stuffed quail eggs, Iranian caviar, stuffed rack of roast lamb, roast peacock, fig rings, raspberry sweet champagne sherbet, and of course the most expensive wines. The estimated cost for the gathering? Approximately $3 million.

39. The most expensive car ever built was the US presidential 1969 Lincoln Continental Executive of which the US Secret Service took delivery in 1968. It is 21 feet long with a 13.4-foot wheel base, has two tons of armour plating and weighs 5.35 tons. Its cost was estimated at $500,000 and even in the event of all four tyres being blown out it could still travel at 50 m.p.h.!

silly stories about paying or being paid money

1. Mr John Chandler of Bristol received an account from the local electricity board. He had only just moved into his house that day and barely turned on the lights. The electricity account was for precisely £0.00 pence. He, not unnaturally, ignored it.

One month later he received a red copy of the same account stating that he owed the computer at the Electricity Board £0.00 pence. He giggled and ignored it again.

A week later the board sent him a white postcard, again from the computer, stating that if he did not pay his account within seven days they would cut off his electricity. At this point Mr Chandler stopped giggling and called the board. He was told that it must be a mistake and he should not worry. Seven days later an electricity inspector arrived at his door with instructions to cut off his power. Mr Chandler showed the man the bill for £0.00 pence and they had a good laugh, but two hours later his power was gone.

The next morning Mr Chandler went to the electricity board and delivered a cheque for £0.00 pence.

Three hours later his power was reconnected and the following morning he received a reconnection charge for £25. After a lot of phone calls and hassle Mr Chandler received a letter of apology and the matter was resolved.

A week later he received a gas bill from the Gas Board – the account was for minus £4.50 pence. Mr Chandler sent the bill back together with an invoice on his private company's letterhead for £4.50. Two weeks later a cheque arrived from the Gas Board for £4.50. Two months after this another account arrived from the gas board, this time for minus £38.45. He repeated the game and received another cheque. This went on for a full year, until the Gas Board woke up and sent the gas man round. The gas man fiddled with the meter and informed Mr Chandler that it had been running backwards for the past twelve months. Mr Chandler is the only known human being to have made a profit out of the British Gas Board!

2. Mr John Smith (name changed to protect the guilty) applied for three different credit cards, for each of six different names, all aliases, at six different (all disused) addresses in London. He had also opened, six months before, six bank accounts using his original bank account to provide the references. Through these accounts he regularly paid small sums of money, from one to another, keeping always strictly in credit and operating the accounts on his best behaviour.

Three weeks after his applications, the eighteen different credit cards arrived at the false addresses and Mr Smith collected them. He also had twelve complete chequebooks, two from each false account, and six cheque cards which would guarantee cheques up to fifty pounds. Mr Smith then took a holiday abroad.

He went to southern Italy where he had been some months before to check out one or two banks. At certain banks in the south of Italy, the bank clerks don't bother to ask for a passport when a foreign visitor cashes cheques, and it was to these banks that our Mr Smith went. Over a couple of weeks he cashed all 360 cheques, travelling quietly around from bank to bank, day in and day out. Unlike the UK, the European banks also don't trouble to mark the back of the chequebook when a cheque is cashed, and it is also possible to cash two cheques at a time at most Italian banks.

In addition Mr Smith cashed money on his various credit cards and with the American Express card he bought jewellery and saleable goods.

By the end of his stay he had accumulated £56,000 in cash. This he changed, as he went along, into Swiss francs, sterling and dollars. At the end of his stay he travelled to Switzerland where he deposited the cash in three banks, leaving himself sufficient money to fly back to the UK, where he went the rounds of the British banks and cashed more money with the cards. He then disposed of the cards and flew away. Mr Smith has never flown back again.

It must be added that banks and credit card companies, as a result of this type of fraud, are tightening up on their procedures in Europe and it would now be almost impossible to play Mr Smith's game again.

3. Mr P. D. James of New York City went down to his mail box in his apartment building on the Upper West Side of Manhattan and collected his mail one bright spring morning. Amongst the letters was a bank statement. Mr James was not doing particularly well with his small export business and on such a pleasant morning he did not wish to spoil the day by opening the letter.

Later in the day, however, his conscience got the better of him and he opened the buff envelope. To his absolute astonishment, his account was $32,800 in credit. Poring over the figures he discovered that there was a direct debit payment to his account for $34,000, with a code number before it. In effect, therefore, his worst fears were confirmed – he was actually overdrawn up to his limit. The rest of the day was depressing as Mr James felt convinced that the mistake would soon be rectified. The following month, after Mr James had forgotten about his windfall, the usual statement arrived. He feared that this time, as he had been unable to pay very much into his account, it would be accompanied by a bank letter demanding that he put his account in order. Instead the figure shown was $61,763 in credit. Another direct debit with the same code for $34,000 had been credited to his account. This put Mr James in a great dilemma for he knew that if he drew the situation to the attention of his bank they would certainly withdraw the money. What if the mistake didn't matter? The money, after all, could have come through some computer error from a source which might never notice it. Mr James waited another month, without spending any of the money. Sure enough on the next statement the credit had gone up another $34,000. He was now the proud but uneasy owner of just under $100,000. Mr James wrote a cheque for the full credit amount, paid it into another bank account, moved apartments and breathed silently. The following month he went back to his old apartment building to pick up his mail. His old bank account was up another $34,000. He wrote another cheque.

Three years later Mr James is a dollar millionaire,

has closed his account at the first bank and now lives in the Bahamas!

4. On 7 May 1824 Beethoven was present at the first performance of his 9th Symphony – his greatest and most monumental work. He sat in the orchestra and followed the score, for by then he was totally deaf. At the end of the performance he believed the symphony to have been a failure until a friend turned him around to see the audience in thunderous applause. The net profit of the 9th Symphony for Beethoven was approximately $60.

During the year 1982 alone the EMI record company grossed £520,000 from Beethoven's works.

5. In 1974 in the small English parish of Bramber the local council voted to economize on electricity by going without electric lighting in the local streets for three days. At the end of the three days it was proudly announced that there had been a saving of £11.59 from the sacrifice. However, it was also announced that turning off the lights at the beginning of the three days and turning them on again at the end had cost £30.48. It had therefore cost the council £18.89 to spend three days in darkness.

6. On 28 July 1962 the Mariner 1 space probe was launched from Cape Canaveral, en route for Venus. Its first step was to booster speed up to 25,820 m.p.h., after 44 minutes 9200 solar cells were to unfold, 80 days later a computer would calculate the final course corrections and after 100 days the craft would circle Venus and scan the mysterious clouds surrounding it.

However, as it transpired, none of this happened and the vessel plunged into the Atlantic Ocean only four minutes after take off. Enquiries later revealed that a minus sign had been omitted from the instructions fed into the computer. 'It was a human error,' a launch spokesman said. This human error – minus a minus sign – cost £4,280,000!

7. In August 1977 a Dutch vet was required to treat an ailing cow. To investigate its internal gases he inserted a tube into its anus and struck a match. The jet of flame set fire to some bales of hay and then the entire farm, causing damage estimated at £45,000. The vet was fined £140 and the cow escaped, suffering from shock.

8. Three thieves in Billericay, Essex, carefully planned a post office robbery, setting up their armoury, getaway cars and donning heavy disguises. The only detail they failed to check was the post office they planned to rob, which had been closed for twelve years. Upon arrival they discovered the premises to be a small local shop where, on demanding money from the till, they were handed £6.00.

9. In 1967 a Nigerian labourer altered his pay cheque from £9. 4s to £697,000 – and 4 shillings. His forgery was successful until he entered a bank and demanded that the cheque be cashed.

16

random and totally unconnected facts about money

1. When Mrs (First Lady) Nancy Reagan first moved into the White House in 1981 she spent $209,000 on crockery alone.

2. In the unstable economy of Chile, after the coup which deposed Salvador Allende (a coup which took place because of the dreadful inflationary problems of the country) the new ruler, Pinochet, was witness to an increase in the cost of living during one single month of 212 per cent.

3. In 1979 a pair of Judy Garland's false eyelashes were auctioned and sold for $125.

4. Richard the Lion Heart, while on one of his notorious money-hunting sieges, received a mortal arrow wound, and while slowly expiring, he spoke to the archer who had delivered the great king towards his maker, saying 'I forgive you'. And then to his soldiers, who had the fellow captive: 'Take off his chains, give him one hundred shillings and let him go.'

5. Czar Peter I of Russia (1672–1725) levied a rather curious tax on his people – charging 100 roubles to everyone with a beard.

6. In 1963 the Egyptian statues of the God-King Rameses II faced destruction from the rising waters of the Aswan Dam. The three statues, counted as some of the world's greatest treasures, had to be moved nearly 700 feet further up the rock face overlooking Lake Nasser. The statues are 3200 years old and a Swedish engineer devised a method of breaking down the statues into over 1000 pieces, some weighing over 30 tons. He managed the task over a period of 4 1/2 years at a cost of £16,600,000.

7. The famous Roman roads, built by order of the Emperor Augustus, stretched over a total of fifty thousand miles between the Persian Gulf and the Humber in Britain. Letters could be delivered at terrific speed, messenger riders covering as much as 200 miles in a day. But the roads were not cheap by Roman standards – they cost the equivalent of £5500 for the Roman mile (nine tenths of the modern mile). The modern motorway costs around £1 million a mile, and look how long they last by comparison!

8. Sydney's infamous Opera House was planned to be completed over a period of two years at a cost of £5 million. In fact, due to 'unforeseen circumstances' the job took fourteen years and cost £50 million plus. One of the biggest problems was the shells which formed the roof – when the designer prepared them he found they could not be supported and had to build giant arches as well as increasing the bulk of the shells to a weight of over 28,000 tons.

9. The biggest rubbish recycling plant in the world has been built in Nashville, Tennessee. The trash is burnt and the energy released is used to power thirty-eight office blocks in the city. The total cost of the plant was $16.5 million.

10. The modern bra was first conceived by a New York lady who, tired of the restrictive corsets of the

age (1914) constructed the first brassiere out of two handkerchiefs and some ribbon. Many of her friends copied the idea but she was unable to market the concept successfully herself and so sold the idea to a corset company for £15,000. That same company has since received a total of $15 million purely for patent fees from other corporations marketing the bra.

11. If you wish to take the chance on being revived after death, you can have your body frozen into cryogenic suspension. The cost of immortality (expectation) is between £3000 and £6000 (presumably

Cryogenic suspension

depending on the degree of comfort or the length of freeze time!) and an annual charge of £300 for storage. Make sure you leave enough behind for a couple of hundred years because if the standing order should stop, the result could be a bit smelly.

12. In 1771 a Dr James Graham was the rage of London society with his magnetic and electrical cures. He opened a special health clinic called The Temple of Health which invited people to have special baths attended by nubile black girls and a scantily clad Emma Hart (later Nelson's mistress Lady Hamilton) who would flit about the 'patients' as an example of glowing health. The greatest attraction of the Temple was the magnetic bed which encouraged childless couples to conceive because of the 'ever circulating magnetic current' – the charge was £500 a night – in those days! The venerable doctor eventually returned to his home town, Edinburgh, where he was placed in a lunatic asylum/gaol.

13. Jack Swimmer – a paint manufacturer – predicted in 1956, a month before the election of Dwight D. Eisenhower, that the votes cast in his favour would be 1,218,462 for Los Angeles, 2,875,637 for California and 33,974,241 for the whole country. He sealed up the envelope with the predictions in it, together with $5000 to be given to charity if he was wrong. The envelope was placed in a box inside another box in a bank vault with an armed guard until the election. The results of the election were precisely those predicted by Swimmer – to the very last number. He was so delighted that he gave the money to charity anyway. He was also responsible for an accurate prediction of the 1952 election and of a World Series baseball result.

34

14. In Minnesota in 1936 a prize of $100 was offered to anyone who could think of a name for a new kind of cheap meat to be tinned and marketed. The winning entry was derived from two words – SPiced hAM – SPAM.

15. The Japanese name tsunami means a tidal wave which follows an earthquake – a particularly nasty type of tidal wave. One of the largest ever recorded occurred off the coast of Hawaii, having travelled 2250 miles in $4\frac{1}{2}$ hours at 490 m.p.h. It caused the death of 173 people and £50 million worth of damage to the island.

16. The most disastrous lightning storm occurred in California in 1926, raging for four days and covering 900 acres of land, causing $15 million worth of damage but killing only two people.

gamblers anonymous

The biggest and best gambling wins, past and present throughout the world and, just to give balance, some of the biggest losses too.

1. One of the biggest, more recent gambling competitions, which was started by the London *Daily Mail* and picked up by other Fleet Street tabloids, gave away a top prize of £1 million. At time of writing, one of the prizes has been won.

2. The largest ever amount won on the British football pools to date is £953,874 won by David Preston of Burton-on-Trent on 23 February 1980. Mr Preston won £804,573.35 from Littlewood's Pools and £149,300.75 from Vernon's Pools.

3. Super Bertha is an enormous Las Vegas slot machine which is said to pay out $1 million once in every 25,000 million plays.

4. One of the lesser-known Saudi princes is said to have lost $1 million in a single roulette session in Las Vegas in December 1974.

5. The richest horse race ever held is the All-American Futurity in New Mexico. The 1982 prizes totalled nearly $2 million.

6. In 1983 a group of three life insurance salesmen formed a 'system' to beat a large London club roulette wheel. The system was based on small bets, made regularly over a long period, working to larger amounts. Over the first month they netted winnings of £38,000 by this method. In the second month their net profits increased to £59,000. In the third month they lost all they had won and a further £23,000 before giving up the 'system'.

7. Mr Arthur Kaluna, an immigrant from eastern Europe, settled in Germany with very little money and no prospect of work. In the first two months he entered five British competitions which he saw advertised in UK newspapers and magazines. He won first prize in all five competitions and his winnings included £17,500 in cash, two brand new cars, both of which he sold, a complete stereo unit worth £3000 which he also sold and a set of crystal glasses. The net income derived from his luck was £32,350.54. He returned to his homeland and was never heard of again.

8. Mrs Betty Harris is one of hundreds of professional competition punters. Mrs Harris spends her whole life entering every single competition she can possibly find and also, of course goes to bingo every week. Mrs Harris earns, on average, each year, in excess of £25,000 in cash or prize value plus a huge quantity of goods she cannot realize, such as one hundred and fifty-two coffee percolators, sixteen electric toasters, forty-eight blankets, seventeen hundred-weight of oranges, eight tents, and fifty-six pieces of various leather wear.

9. Anthony James Pretty attended the reading of his father's will, a successful and locally notorious gambler in the casinos of Monte Carlo. The will provided that Anthony could either receive £500 immediately or he could follow a number of clues which would lead to a hoard of treasure. The treasure was worth £2 million. If he took the £500 the treasure would remain buried. Anthony Pretty drove home, got out of his car and while walking across his back garden to avoid some building work being done on his house, tripped in the dark on a garden hoe and broke his elbow on a metal box containing the treasure buried just below the surface. He had taken the £500 option.

10. Ladbroke's, the world's largest bookmaker, turned over £552 million during 1981 from its 1249 shops.

11. The world's biggest gambling win was made in the Pennsylvania weekly Lotto game on 19 June 1982 by an unnamed player who won $5.5 million.

12. Here's a sad story that defines the phallacy [*sic*] of money and its power to give happiness: William Bergstrom, a confirmed gambler, won $1,308,000 on the potent dice of the casinos during 1984 – an astonishing win in the history of gambling. Equally astonishing was his loss of $1,000,000 on a single throw of the same dice some time later, making Nevada history with his ridiculous gesture. He was found dead in a Las Vegas hotel in early 1985, having committed suicide at the age of thirty-three. What a karma he'll have!

common excuses for not paying money

Anyone who has been through penury, bankruptcy or even a 'low ebb', will know this list of answers well. The most adept of excuse makers are small business proprietors who rely heavily on generous cash flow to survive. The big companies pay late so the small businessman must stretch his credit at the other end. This means that all small businesses are constantly chasing one another to pass on money around the table – one to the other. It's a bit concertina-like. If one company paid on time, then theoretically the

whole chain might catch up. Meanwhile here are the forty-four most common excuses gathered from about two hundred people.

1. Broke, skint, busted, bankrupt.
2. Don't get paid till next week.
3. Cheque's in the post.
4. Cheque's lost in the post.
5. Sorry, forgot to sign cheque.
6. Bank's closed.
7. Missed the last post.
8. All the directors are out, can't get a signature.
9. Lack of funds.
10. Stock-taking.
11. Chequebook lost.
12. No cheques left.
13. Only one cheque left, needed it to buy food over weekend.
14. The machine gobbled up my card.
15. The dog ate my card.
16. The dog ate my chequebook.
17. The dog ate me.
18. Cash-flow problems.
19. The recession got me.
20. The computer's down.
21. The computer's just up.
22. The Guvnor's at lunch.
23. Money's on three-month deposit.
24. Somebody else stole the cheque I sent you – we're trying to trace who.
25. My secretary put the wrong address on the envelope.
26. The envelope came back, I'll mail it again.
27. Keep all me assets in equities, old chap.
28. Me mother's sick, hospital bills, ya know.
29. Insurance claim hasn't come through.

30. Dear oh dear, must have left the wallet at home.
31. Dear oh dear, must have left the wife at home.
32. My agent hasn't paid me yet.
33. I'm resting. (Common in the acting profession.)
34. Sorry old chap, simply haven't got it.
35. Market's a bit low just now.
36. Spent it.
37. The cat peed all over it.
38. The baby chewed it up.
39. The insurance man came last night.
40. The book-keeper's sick.
41. The accountant's done a bunk with the money.
42. The chairman's done a bunk with the money.
43. Lost it on the wheel.
44. Can't think what happened, must have sent it to the wrong address.

common and uncommon places where people keep their money

People are funny about where they keep their money. First they generally don't want anyone to know where it is; this is a kind of security/privacy impulse brought about by deep psychological complexes connected with sex, early pot training etc., and second the place a person chooses to keep their money will tell you a lot about what sort of person they are. People who keep money under the mattress, in a sock, up the chimney or similar places, don't trust anyone – least of all those, like banks, who profess to be trustworthy. Someone who tells you he keeps his money abroad is either very rich and trying to avoid paying tax or lying in preparation for the day when someone asks him to pay a bill. Naturally, money abroad takes weeks and months to bring back. Mostly though, if you ask someone where they keep their money you are likely to get the same answer – 'mind your own business' – which seems fair enough.

1. The bank.
2. The building society.
3. On deposit.
4. In shares.
5. In a safe.
6. In equities.
7. In insurance.
8. In the post office.
9. Under the bed.
10. Under the mattress.
11. In gold.
12. In a sock.
13. In a pension fund.
14. In a shoe box.
15. In perpetuity.
16. Buried in the garden.
17. In property.
18. In a business.
19. Abroad.
20. In unit trusts.
21. In bonds.
22. In gilts.
23. In a back pocket.
24. In land.
25. In a bank vault.
26. In antiques.
27. In art.

10

pleasant things that can happen to people because of money or the lack of it

1. *Enlightenment.* When you need money most, very often it isn't there, and when you can do without it, money arrives out of nowhere – those who become enlightened to this fact will have fun, presumably whether they have money or not.

2. *Love.* Falling in love probably means you spend more – on making yourself look better, or making your new lover look better. A need to spend it produces a need to make it, and when you've got it, you get rid of it faster. Love makes the world go round.

3. *Sex.* Too little sex will make you greedy. Too much sex will make you hungry. Either way, money follows.

4. *Rolls-Royces.* There is nothing in the world like a Roller; everyone should drive one for a day – all sorts of pleasant things happen when you do. Keep your eyes on the road and everybody's eyes will be on you.

5. *Freedom.* Money will only produce freedom if you know what it is like not to have it and not care. Money and worry are as bad as no money and worry.

6. *Presidency.* Presidents smile a lot, not because they have money, though this may help them get there, but because they know that they'll probably be dead the next day – this accounts for the slightly sick look that follows each smile!

7. *Wisdom.* Comes from dealing with problems. Money comes from dealing with problems profitably.

8. *Admiration.* From those who don't have money. Those that do know how others got it.

9. *Winning.* The pleasure derived from winning is greater the more often you lose. Theoretically, therefore, one win at the end of a lifetime of losses would be the best!

10. *Comfort.* Can be pleasant so long as you like to sit down.

unpleasant things that can happen to people because of money or the lack of it

1. Bankruptcy.	**12.** G.B.H.
2. Alcoholism.	**13.** Hit and run.
3. Drug addiction.	**14.** Phone cut off.
4. Divorce.	**15.** Power cut off.
5. Love.	**16.** Foreclosure.
6. Suicide.	**17.** Beriberi.
7. Bailiffs.	**18.** Kidnapping.
8. Marriage.	**19.** Begging letters.
9. Fraud.	**20.** Greed.
10. Jail.	**21.** Lunacy.
11. Murder.	**22.** Jehovah's Witnesses.

23. Depression.
24. Loneliness.
25. Starvation.
26. Writs.
27. Success.
28. Failure.
29. Heart disease.
30. Premature ageing.
31. Anorexia nervosa.
32. Overeating.
33. Political ambition.
34. Scandal.
35. Life insurance.
36. Mortgages.
37. Hiccoughs.
38. Psychoanalysis.
39. Tedium.
40. Catastrophe.

things that people hate to spend money on

1. Rates.
2. Taxes.
3. School fees.
4. Ex-wives.
5. Mothers-in-law.
6. Kid brothers.
7. Elder sisters.
8. Operations.
9. Dry cleaning.
10. Laundry.
11. Parking fines.
12. Insurance policies.
13. Bills of any kind.
14. Plumbers.
15. Roof menders.
16. Door to door salesmen.
17. Batteries.
18. Car repairs.
19. Legal fees.
20. Accountants.
21. Lawyers.
22. Sex.
23. Charities.
24. School rulers.
25. Sweets for kids.
26. Dog food.
27. Toilet paper.
28. Anything that's boring.
29. Dentists.
30. Underpants.
31. Vests.
32. Wellington boots.

33. Goldfish food.
34. Funerals.
35. Washing powder.
36. Fish cakes.
37. Haggis.

38. Cabbies.
39. Bus and Underground fares.
40. Muggers.

things people love to spend money on

1. Furs.
2. Cars.
3. Houses.
4. Lovers.
5. Birthdays.
6. Christmas.
7. Parties.
8. Booze.
9. Cigarettes.
10. Tomorrow.
11. Gambling.
12. Mums.
13. Pretty girls.
14. Daughters.
15. Fathers.
16. Books on money!
17. Best sellers.
18. Movies.
19. Soap.
20. Flowers.
21. Perfume.
22. Presents.
23. Jewellery.
24. Tea at Fortnum and Mason.
25. Clothes.
26. Antiques.
27. Trinkets.
28. Holidays.
29. Boats.
30. Toffee.
31. Black Magic chocolates.
32. Any kind of chocolates.
33. Excitement.
34. Decorations.
35. Bedrooms.
36. Shoes.
37. TVs.
38. Videos.
39. Tapes.
40. Cakes.

40

things people never spend money on

1. Dead cats.
2. Dead budgerigars.
3. Cigarette ends.
4. Gossip.
5. Toenails.
6. Ear wax.
7. Agents.
8. Ants (except the French).
9. Frogs (except the French).
10. The French (even the French).
11. Aborigines.
12. Collections for parking-meter attendants.
13. Dog shit.
14. Bullshit.
15. Rain.
16. Lightning.
17. Wind.
18. The wind.
19. Pubic hair.
20. Milk bottles.
21. Walking.
22. Abuse.
23. Sludge.
24. Snot.
25. Barf.
26. Flies.
27. Smegma.
28. Wild flowers.
29. Mud.
30. Losers.
31. Jinxes.
32. Quicksands.
33. Clouds.
34. Dandruff (getting rid of it yes, but who buys dandruff?)
35. Muggers.
36. Rapists.
37. Grafitti.
38. Jehovah's Witnesses.
39. Cat pee.
40. Hiccoughs.

Section Two

FAME AND FORTUNE

Some people are content to go out into the marketplace and make their money quietly and without the whole world knowing of it – there are enough problems in this. There are others, though, who would do it and have the world know of every move and every penny they make. As if making a fortune were not hazardous enough – they would have fame too.

22

of the biggest world
money earners

Because of various rules of discretion it is often difficult to discover the highest earners throughout the world, but here is a list of 22 of the big money earners.

1. The greatest fortune gathered in the sports world was made by Muhammad Ali Haj between 1960 and 1981, from boxing. His total earnings were estimated to be $69 million.

2. The highest-paid bullfighter ever was El Cordobes who became a millionaire in 1965. In 1970 he received approximately £750,000 for 121 fights.

3. The most successful jockey ever was Willie Shoemaker who, from March 1949 to June 1982 rode 8136 winners earning $87,951,800 in prize money for their owners.

4. The highest-earning tennis player is Bjorn Borg who won $1,019,345 in 1979 alone. The highest female tennis earnings were made by Martina Navratilova in 1981 at $865,437.

5. The highest-earning artist of all time was Pablo Picasso, who sold many hundreds of paintings during his lifetime. Two examples would be *Two Brothers* and *Seated Harlequin* which sold for the highest price ever made by an artist for his paintings while still alive – $1,950,000.

6. The highest price ever paid for the work of a living sculptor is $1,265,000 for *Reclining Figure* by Henry Moore.

7. One of the highest-paid authoresses was Judith Krantz, who in 1979 received the greater part of $3,208,875 for the rights to her book *Princess Daisy*.

8. Another of the world's highest-earning fiction writers is Jacqueline Susann who has sold over 25 million copies of just one of her novels – *Valley of the Dolls*.

9. One of the highest-earning musicians was – and still is – Wladziu Valentino Liberace who has earned in excess of $2 million each twenty-six-week season and as much as $150,000 for one night's performance in the US.

10. Enrico Caruso died worth $9,000,000.

11. The highest-paid songwriter is still Paul McCartney with more than forty-three million-seller songs to his credit.

12. Bing Crosby is estimated to have sold in excess of half a billion records in his lifetime, though there are no published figures as to his earnings from these sales.

13. The largest TV contract ever signed was with Marie Osmond and NBC in 1981 for $7 million.

14. The biggest-earning hotel chain is Holiday Inns Inc., with a 1981 income of $4,300,000,000 from 1750 hotels including over 300,000 rooms in nearly sixty countries. The first Holiday Inn was opened in 1952.

15. The biggest-earning grocery-store chain is Safeways with 1981 revenues of $16,580,318,000 from 2477 stores and 160,000 employees.

16. In 1983 a single man earned, from a single financial transaction, the sum of $234 million – in Europe. Unfortunately his name is not available for publication!

17. The largest fizzy-drink manufacturer is Coca-Cola which sells approximately 250 million drinks a day.

18. The highest-paid model was Cheryl Tiegs who was put under contract by Noxell, the cosmetics group, for five years at $1,500,000 for the rights to her face for that period.

19. The highest-reported salary paid to a single businessman was in 1981 to Mr Roland Genin – the sum of $5,658,000.

20. One of the highest-paid monarchs in history is Queen Elizabeth II who received the following remuneration from the Civil List in 1983:

Wages	£2,523,000	Gratuities	30,000
Food	255,000	Staff travel	30,000
Garden parties	140,000	Presents	30,000
Horses	85,000	Gardens	25,000
Household	75,000	Chapels	25,000
Cellars	70,000	Medals, cups	20,000
Cars	55,000	Rents and rates	10,000
Laundry	45,000	Newspapers	8,000
Flowers	40,000	Library	5,000
Castle expenses	40,000	Sundries	69,000
Liveries	30,000	TOTAL	£3,610,000

21. By contrast to the British Queen, the head of state of the United Arab Emirates, Shaikh Zayid ibn Sultan an-Nuhayan, has title to some $9000 million of his country's gross product.

22. Al Capone can lay claim to the highest income received in history in one year by a single individual – an estimated $105 million during 1927.

very, very rich people

In this decade it would be ill advised for any author to put down in print the true identity of the richest people in the world – even if it were possible to find out. People with very large fortunes tend to remain hidden, for very good reasons. Certainly the most publicized billionaires are not the richest people in the world. Most of the enormous fortunes are owned by trusts belonging, several times removed, to Arab families, and mentioning them in a book of lists would be boring and pointless. But there is a lot of fun to be had looking at the ways the very rich have used their money.

1. The best-known dollar billionaire in history was Daniel K. Ludwig, born in Michigan, US, in 1897. At the age of eighty in 1977 he was estimated to be worth $3 billion. Subsequently, owing to some unhappy investments made later in his life (!) he became an ex-billionaire but in the official records no one has yet been recorded as having as much money as he had.

To bring his fortune into perspective, Mr Ludwig could have done the following with his money:

– Paid for the entire Falklands War two and a half times over.

– Bought out the entire assets of the Royal Bank of Scotland today.

– Given a dollar bill to every living human being and still had change left over.

– Given every new-born human being a dollar bill from 1 January 1977 to 1 January 2018.

– Paid the salary of the average university lecturer for 192,307 years.

2. Haroldson Lafayette Hunt of Dallas, Texas, is quoted in the *Guinness Book of Records* as being one of the world's richest private citizens. In the 1968 edition of *Guinness* he is stated to have had an annual income of $50 million, but following that record H. L. Hunt made the decision to allow his son to inherit his fortune.

Nelson Bunker Hunt is so infamous in financial circles now that if you're a Texan and you wish to borrow money from any of the major lenders, the first question that's asked is 'Were you ever associated with Bunker Hunt?' The answer will determine your eligibility!

Bunker Hunt, in partnership with the royal family of Saudi Arabia, was responsible, early in 1980, for what is now known as the Great Silver Bubble.

The idea was that Bunker Hunt, in partnership with Prince Abdullah of Saudi Arabia, put together a fortune amounting to between $500 million and $1 billion to buy the largest portion of the world silver market that has ever been cornered by two individuals in the history of the world. Their intention was to take the silver physically, using large carrier aircraft, to Switzerland, and hold it until the price of silver rose to $25 per ounce, which they expected to happen in late 1979 or early 1980. Because of the manner in which world events change the values of metal, the price did not rise at the rate expected and as Bunker had bought silver through the 'futures' market, he was committed to buy it at prices that were beyond his expectations. He was therefore unable to meet his obligations and the result produced a slump in the market and a colossal loss in the Bunker Hunt and Saudi family accounts.

3. Ray Kroc, at the age of fifty, was selling paper cups for $35 a week and playing the piano part time to supplement his income. Twenty-five years later, he spent his money on making 25 billion hamburgers and was the owner and builder of McDonald's Golden Arches Restaurants – the largest and fastest-growing fast-food company in the world. From 1954 to 1976 the McDonald organization, under Kroc's direction, increased from one store to 4177. By 31 March 1984 there were 7819 stores. Not bad for a paper-cup salesman.

4. Henrietta Howland Green (1835–1916) was renowned for only one thing – miserliness. She was said to be the meanest woman who ever lived. At her death the estate was valued at $95 million and she had $31,400,000 in one bank account alone. Her will was found in a tin box with four pieces of soap, and she was said to have delayed an operation on her son's leg for so long, in an attempt to find a free hospital, that the leg had to be amputated. She was said to live off cold porridge because she was too mean to heat it up, and died of an attack of apoplexy over an argument concerning the virtues of skimmed milk!

5. A well-known invocation – James Gordon Bennett – (1841–1918), was also renowned for his extravagant generosity. Amongst his various vices was a passion for mutton chops and once he had found the restaurant in Monte Carlo which served mutton chops to his liking, he visited every day. On one morning, however, he found his favourite table occupied by some happy drinkers. He went to the proprietor and offered to buy the place at any price. The price asked was $40,000 (about $240,000 now), and once Bennett had paid up the imbibers were asked to leave. He settled down to his favourite meal at his favourite table and during the meal gave the restaurant to the waiter who served him on condition that the table be reserved permanently for him, and that the mutton chops always be prepared by the same chef.

facts about the very poor

1. Every year the US government computes a series of figures which it terms 'the poverty threshold'. Anyone with an income under this figure is classified as 'poor'. These individuals are eligible for food stamps, Medicaid services and other 'benefits'. Single people under sixty-five were 'poor' in 1981 if their annual income was less than $4729. For a family of two the poverty line was $5917; for three, $7250; for four, $9287. It was estimated that 11.2 per cent of all families were below this poverty line.

2. In India, the average annual incomes for 1981 were:

A trained factory worker $1772
A semi-skilled worker $1328
An unskilled worker $886
A clerk $708
A driver $638
A full-time house servant $326

3. Just to compare the two countries: if you took a walk down Madison Avenue and hung a left into 52nd Street, you might find a great little restaurant, typical in style and price for New York, where you could buy 'two eggs, fried up, bacon, toast, sausage, coffee' for around $3.00. Alternatively, on a trip from say Bombay to Poona, the cab driver might stop by a small roadside shack where you could buy exactly the same meal every day for two weeks, for a total cost of $3.00!

4. In Britain there is only one way to measure the breadline and that is on the basis of the government's 'gifts' to those in need. If you've paid all your National Insurance stamps and are a single person living at home, you're entitled to the lowest level of benefit – £27.05 per week. If you have never paid any stamps, for example if you're a student, living with parents at home, you can get Supplementary Benefit which is a real 'gift' amounting to £21.45 per week plus £3.10 per week towards the cost of paying your parents' rent. If you have a wife and five kids living with you in your parents' home, things may not look too good generally, but the government will help you out to

Fried up

the tune of £16.70 per week for the wife and fifteen pence for each child! Well, at least you could buy them a Mars Bar every Friday – just.

years of rising cinema costs

Year	US	UK
1935	24 cents	10d
1936	25 cents	10d
1937–9	23 cents	10d
1940–42	25 cents	11d
1943	29 cents	1s 4d
1944–6	33 cents	1s 5d
1947–9	38 cents	1s 5d
1950–52	50 cents	1s 8d
1952–6	65 cents	2s 4d
1957–61	70 cents	2s 10d
1961–5	85 cents	3s 4d
1966–7	$1.19	4s 5d
1967–70	$1.55	6s 1d
1971–4	$1.88	50p
1972–5	$2.05	61p
1976–8	$2.34	83p
1979–80	$2.46	£1.14
1983	$5.00	£3.25
1985	$6.50	£4.25

movies and their gross rental income

Despite the arrival of the flourishing video market, the cinema still makes some of the biggest revenues in the world. In fact, during 1983 and 1984 films have grossed greater figures than ever before. Every year *Variety* publishes the 'All-Time Film Rental Champs' and the following list is their top thirty. For true movie buffs the actual published list is a lot longer and can be found in their *78th Show Business Annual*.

Title	Director	Total Rental $US
1. *E.T. The Extra Terrestrial*	Spielberg	209,567,000
2. *Star Wars*	Lucas	193,500,000
3. *Return of the Jedi*	Marquand	165,500,000
4. *The Empire Strikes Back*	Kershner	141,600,000
5. *Jaws*	Spielberg	133,435,000
6. *Raiders of the Lost Ark*	Spielberg	115,598,000
7. *Grease*	Kleiser	96,300,000
8. *Tootsie*	Pollack	94,571,613
9. *The Exorcist*	Friedkin	89,000,000
10. *The Godfather*	Coppola	86,275,000
11. *Close Encounters of the Third Kind*	Spielberg	83,452,000
12. *Superman*	Donner	82,800,000
13. *The Sound of Music*	Wise	79,748,000
14. *The Sting*	Hill	79,419,900
15. *Gone with the Wind*	Fleming	76,700,000

16. *Saturday Night Fever*	Badham	74,100,000
17. *National Lampoon's Animal House*	Landis	74,000,000
18. *Nine to Five*	Higgins	66,200,000
19. *Rocky III*	Stallone	65,763,177
20. *Superman II*	Lester	65,100,000
21. *On Golden Pond*	Rydell	63,000,000
22. *Kramer vs Kramer*	Benton	61,734,000
23. *Smokey and The Bandit*	Needham	61,055,000
24. *One Flew Over the Cuckoo's Nest*	Forman	59,205,793
25. *Stir Crazy*	Poitier	58,408,000
26. *American Graffiti*	Lucas	56,662,000
27. *Star Trek*	Wise	56,000,000
28. *Rocky*	Avildsen	55,921,424
29. *Jaws II*	Szwarc	55,608,000
30. *An Officer and a Gentleman*	Hackford	55,223,000

It's easy to see, just from this list, why Spielberg and Lucas dominate the Hollywood popularity polls. Spielberg's contribution so far tops the half-billion-dollar mark and Lucas is just under the same figure.

creative pay-packets

The best-documented payrolls are those of the movie stars and movie companies. Everyone knows by now stories like Marlon Brando's record breaking earnings for *The Formula* in which he made $2,750,000 for some eleven days' work, or his massive earnings on the movie *Superman*. But not so much is generally available in the creative world as a whole – TV actors, interviewers, musicians etc. So, here is a random list of some pay cheques in the uncertain world of creativity.

1. In Australia the most successful TV and radio personality, John Laws, recently signed a five-year contract for £2.6 million.

2. Johnny Carson, one of the best-known TV personalities in the world, has an income which can only be estimated, ranging from $3 million to $6 million per annum – and this does not count $250,000 a night for personal appearances plus payments for promotional deals.

3. Alan Alda, the founder member of *M*A*S*H*, makes around $5 million a year from the series which, not too long ago, was being shown on television in the States roughly three times a day!

4. If Wolfgang Amadeus Mozart had lived longer his amazingly prolific rate of composition would have made him one of the richest composers of music. During his short thirty-five-year life he composed 1000 operas, operettas, symphonies, violin sonatas and concertos – of which only seventy were published before his death. Royalties from the many recordings which have since been published and recorded exceed £24 million since his death in 1791.

5. One of the highest-paid performers of classical music during the twentieth century was pianist Ignace Paderewski (1860–1941). As well as being prime minister of Poland he accumulated over $5 million from performance fees.

6. The highest-paid opera singer was Enrico Caruso (1873–1921) who died worth $9 million.

7. One of the poorest-paid classical singers was Mr Charles Baintree of Southwold who between 1972 and 1981 gave eighteen performances in the streets of London and received from ungenerous passers-by the net sum of £72.52.

8. One of the highest-paid stuntmen in show business is Dan Robinson who received $100,000 for one 1000-foot leap without a parachute and survived.

stars' insurance

Many of the great movie stars have paid high premiums to protect their most famous parts. Here is a list of the amounts of insurance cover and parts insured.

1. Comedian John Bunny (1863–1915) insured his unlovely face for $1,000,000.

2. Mary Pickford insured her face for the same amount.

3. Charlie Chaplin (1889–1977) insured his feet for $150,000.

4. Clara Kimball Young (1891–1960) insured her 'large and luminous eyes' for $150,000.

5. Ben Turpin (1874–1946) insured his crossed eyes against them becoming uncrossed for $100,000.

6. Edmund Lowe (1890–1971) insured his nose for $35,000.

7. Kathleen Key insured her neck for $25,000.

8. Jimmy Durante insured his nose for a million dollars.

9. Alberta Vaughn insured against the possibility of putting on 20 pounds' weight by June 1927 for $25,000.

10. Walter Hiers insured against losing 45 pounds' weight for $25,000.

11. Betty Grable insured her legs for $1,250,000.

12. Cyd Charisse insured her legs for $10,000,000.

13. Fred Astaire insured his legs for the same amount.

14. Lillian Gish, during the filming of *Way down East*, insured her life for one million dollars.

random facts about movies, stars, directors and their money

1. The total gross income received during 1977 to 1979 from the movie *Star Wars*, directed by George Lucas, was $267 million

2. During 1981 *Superman II* grossed $5,060,000 in a single day in North America.

3. In 1977 James Coburn was paid $500,000 for uttering two words on a series of Schlitz beer commercials – the words were 'Schlitz light'.

4. In 1979 Brooke Shields was paid $250,000 for a one-minute TV commercial by a Japanese company.

5. Faye Dunaway was paid $900,000 for speaking six words on a Japanese department store TV commercial.

6. Barbara Walters of ABC TV in the US receives one million dollars per annum for her work as anchorman for the evening news programme.

7. In 1979 Cheryl Tiegs was paid $1,500,000 for the right to use her face, eyes and lips over a period of five years.

8. TV actor Peter Falk received $350,000 per episode for his performances in *Columbo*.

9. Caroll O'Conner, TV's Archie Bunker, received $200,000 per episode for twenty-four episodes in 1980.

10. Burt Reynolds received $238,095 per day from 20th Century-Fox for his part in *Cannonball Run*.

reasons why Princess Diana is so popular

One of the biggest single assets to arise out of the British system this century is a young woman named Princess Diana, a girl of no great talent, special ability or experience who happened to be the perfect symbol of British royalty and who happened to coax Prince Charles out of bachelordom, and half the rest of the world out of its feeling of lethargy for British royalty. In the past couple of years Princess Di has been seen on more magazine covers and book fronts and in more newspaper reports than any other single human being since Adolf Hitler, and with far better effect!

So here is the list to beat all lists – an assessment of the value to the world of a great princess.

1. The author visited eight different newspaper libraries in London, where records are kept of the newspaper cuttings devoted to Princess Diana during the past year, and measured (using a twelve-inch ruler) the depth of cuttings on record. The total measurement was twenty-two yards deep. This included general reports, dress reports, social functions, general fashion reports, critical comments, baby reports, home activity reports. That comes to approximately one hundred and eighteen thousand, eight hundred cuttings!

2. Women's magazines published in England have on numerous occasions published articles about the princess and where she has either appeared on the front cover or in a major feature article the edition of the magazine in the main has sold out. The total number of copies sold comes to 86 million and the profit for the publishers is approximately £17 million.

3. In the book-publishing world, in the past two years there have been no less than 112 books about or relating to Princess Diana. The total number sold of all these books added together is 27 million, at an average profit to the publishers of 21p per copy sold, totalling an approximate £5,670,000.

4. Taking a somewhat reduced figure to apply to other interested countries such as France, Germany, Holland, Italy and the United States, a fair assessment of the revenues produced over the past two years, from books, magazines and newspapers, would be £12 million.

5. The value of the Princess to the UK as a tourist attraction is another facet of her money-earning capabilities. Three tourist organizations when asked to put a figure on the seductive (tourist-wise that is) powers of Princess Di made a conservative estimate of £7 million, which places her somewhat higher in value than Blackpool Tower, Trafalgar Square and the Houses of Parliament put together.

6. When the princess visits places of value and interest on her various regal tours in the UK, the local merchants enjoy a greatly enhanced income. The figure placed on this aspect of her charisma comes to a grand extra value of £2,800,000.

7. So, conservatively speaking, Princess Diana is worth a cool £44,470,000.

The million-dollar list

Much mystique surrounds the word millionaire. There was a time, not so long ago, when millionaires were quite rare – not so now. Technically an individual can call themselves a millionaire if they either have or own interests in a million dollars or earn one hundred thousand dollars per annum. In the United States during 1983 there were over 5000 tax returns of in excess of $1,000,000 and 450,000 returns in excess of $100,000 – quite a few millionaires. And these were only the ones who admitted to it.

1. Phillip Arthur Mitchell was born in New York City near Greenwich Village in a one-roomed apartment. His father left home when Phillip was five months old and his mother when he was eight. He continued his life in and out of various state schools till the age of fourteen when he took a job as 'gofer' in a taxi company's garage and offices. At eighteen he started to drive the cabs – 'chequers' – in the city, mostly driving at night in the rougher districts. At four a.m. on a Sunday morning Phillip Mitchell dropped off a fare outside the Pierre Hotel whom he had picked up from Harlem. On arriving home he parked the cab outside the apartment of his co-driver who would start work at six and while locking up spotted a bag in the back seat. The bag contained $6,400,000 in bills. Mitchell counted them twice! He got back in the cab and returned to the Pierre where he found the guy who had left the bag of cash. The man was sitting in the lobby of the hotel crying. As Mitchell walked in with the bag the man stood up, embraced Mitchell enthusiastically, dug his hand into the bag and pulled out a huge wad of the bills, asked the porter for another bag and half filled it with dollars. Mitchell walked out of the Pierre Hotel a millionaire.

2. Anthony Price worked on Wall Street as an international commodity broker dealing in precious metal, stones and other commodities such as sugar, cigarettes, and even sheep! He worked hard all his life and struggled for that ultimate goal – to become a millionaire. At thirty-eight years of age he struck lucky with a contract to supply large quantities of an African country's currency to a New York bank which had some use for the money in the US. The contract was worth three million dollars to him in commissions. It took five months to complete with Price working day and night, calling all over the world, working with large legal practices and banks in New York City. He gave his whole energy to it and on the morning of 5 June 1981 the full commission was paid into his bank in midtown Manhattan. At two p.m. he went into the bank to see the manager and be congratulated on his amazing achievement. At 2.05 p.m. three men entered the bank and held up the tellers with shotguns. They had no intention of hurting anyone and the weapons were not loaded. But one of the robbers was attacked by a bank security guard and in the scuffle that followed a shotgun was thrown across the bank, hitting Price on the temple and killing him outright.

3. J. P. Norris won three-quarters of a million pounds on the British football pools. Up until his win he had been earning around £90 per week after tax as a mill hand in the Midlands. First thing he did was to buy his terraced house from the landlord and all the other houses in the road, giving each house, legally, to its tenants. Next he bought the mill where he worked and doubled the wages of the workers there. Within three months the mill was making four times the profit it had made before its change of management. Norris next bought the local cinema and two restaurants in the main town nearby. The week following this purchase spree he won the football pools again – a further £320,000! Just in time to buy another two businesses in the local town.

Five years later, in January 1984 J. P. Norris was a millionaire in his own right from the successful running of the sixteen different businesses he now owns. He still does the football pools each week.

4. Bill Winch spent his entire life with only one ambition – to be a millionaire. From the tender age of five he spoke of money as though it were a religion, mostly encouraged by his father who never earned more than a reasonable wage as a travelling preacher in the United States. Winch Junior grew up in Dallas, Texas, and began working as an oil engineer for one of the large Texas oil-drilling companies, but it was not until he reached the age of fifty-eight that he had managed to amass enough capital to buy and run his own oil business. By this time the oil-drilling world of Texas was on the decline so that his dreams of success were slowly being destroyed as the companies around him gradually went downhill. He managed to hold his own and lived a relatively fruitful life, but refused to be happy with his lot, continuously toiling for this great ambition to top the million-dollar mark in his bank balance and assets. He travelled the world, always complaining and grumbling about how everyone else managed to do it and not him. His faithful wife stuck by him till the end. He was on his death bed, at the age of eighty-two, when his company pulled off a deal with a large export contract to supply materials for Middle East oil companies, and Bill finally became a millionaire. His wife sat beside him as he gently drifted into his final sleep, and broke the news that he had made his life-long ambition and was now officially a millionaire.

'Aren't you pleased William?' she said.

'Pleased?' Bill answered. 'What should I be pleased about – a million dollars ain't worth nothing these days.' Upon which he died.

5. In this modern age of computer technology the opportunity to make large sums of money is available to a new generation of business people. One of the best stories comes from the highly skilled and creative art of computer games where younger and younger technicians are writing programmes for these popular and exciting graphics systems and receiving royalties on their sales by larger marketing consortiums. Peter Ainsworth (name changed) had, at January 1984, written no less than seven hundred different programmes for computer games in the United States and was a millionaire three times over from the resulting sales. The company which markets the games is his own in partnership with his brother who is the expert at putting the packages together and selling them to the retail and wholesale market. Peter Ainsworth is 14 years old!

6. The first self-made millionairess according to the available records was Madame Charles Joseph Walker, née Sarah Breedlove, born in 1867, an uneducated negro orphan who worked as a scrub-woman and who made her fortune from a hair straightener.

7. According to research done by the United States Trust Company in 1980 more than half the US millionaires – 574,342 in all – are millionairesses.

8. The oldest millionairess on record was Mrs Anna Dodge, born in Scotland, who died on 3 June 1970 worth £40,000,000 at the age of 103.

9. The largest amount of money ever given away by a millionaire, or anyone else for that matter, was in the way of bequests handed out by John Davison Rockefeller – totalling some $750,000,000.

10. By contrast, the poorest people in the world are said to be the Tasaday tribe of cave dwellers in central Mindanao, Philippines, who were found in 1971 to have no domesticated animals, agriculture, working utensils, wheels or clothes and certainly no money!

Section Three

MONEY WORDS

The word 'money' was originally associated with the goddess Juno, being minted in her temples in Rome, and through the ages it has continued to be a subject of worship – 'Some men worship rank, some worship power, some worship God, and over all these ideals they dispute – but they all worship money' (Mark Twain).

There are more words in the world's languages to describe money than almost any other subject, excepting possibly sex.

22

words and phrases not in
the dictionaries

1. The man with the pencil
In the money brokerage business, the man with the
pencil is the man who, in one way or another, controls
a fund of money with his signature. He is likely to be
a trustee to a large fund in a bank and with the sweep
of his hand can change lives!

2. Live notes
Live notes refers to securities which are used to pay
interest to those who wish to deposit money on a long-
term basis for interest. The documents of security, or
collateral, are usually issued by a bank and guarantee
the payment of a fixed interest over a period of five,
ten or twenty years, in return for the use of money by
that same bank. Before the money is lodged in the
bank the notes are 'on the shelf', usually with one
banker's signature on them. For the note to become
'live' it must be signed by one or two other bank
officers.

3. Finder
A finder is a person responsible for finding contacts
who have money to lend or securities to buy. The
finder brings the two sides together and is paid a

commission for doing so. If a finder too frequently brings people who do not actually have what the finder says they have, then he will cease to be a finder and become a flake or a scam-artist! (See below.)

4. Arbitrage

This word does have a dictionary definition, in the Penguin Dictionary of Commerce, but in the money market, the dictionary definition does not cover the full meaning at all.

The most specialized area of financial dealing operates a system of arbitrage which is nothing short of a tightrope walk. Money to lend is taken, sometimes in vast quantities, and placed in an intermediary bank, known as a fiduciary bank, where it is matched by securities or collateral. These securities are provided as promissory notes from large banks and pay interest on the money to be borrowed over a fixed period. Normally the period is twenty years and one day. The one day comes from tradition and has no real practical application.

The securities are purchased at a discount price, leaving a surplus, or 'fallout', which is left, rather skilfully, in the hands of the various parties arranging the deal. If the transaction is for say $1,000,000,000 – that's one billion US dollars – then there could be a 'fallout' of as much as $250,000,000. A proportion of this will be returned to the lender as his initial bonus but a certain amount, maybe $50,000,000, will be divided up amongst the 'finders', brokers and collateral providers.

There are numerous pitfalls in such transactions and the nature of the business is highly specialized and subject to every conceivable type of fraud and misrepresentation – but nevertheless people do make their fortunes in this way.

5. A bee

A bee or a B is a billion dollars. The term is not used to describe a billion pounds because no one would ever have a billion pounds! A billion dollars is one thousand million dollars, and a billion pounds is a million million pounds.

6. A daisy-chainer

In the money world, as in many others, people get together because they know other people who know other people, etc. Daisy-chainers are slightly frowned upon because they are part of a long chain of contacts who pass on information, very often totally false, and expect to be paid a commission for introductions which probably have nothing to do with the real deal which is actually happening. Also, daisy-chainers are often responsible for passing bad-mouth gossip down the chain and frequently one can find that information given to one person comes back, a few hours later, totally changed by the daisy chain.

7. Informer

There are numerous people working as brokers in the financial business who are paid and retained by the Inland Revenue or the IRS (Inland Revenue Service – US) or the FBI to inform on individual receipts of money so that the various authorities can claim tax. The FBI have been known to plant agents in hotel lobbies in the cities like Zurich or London, where much of the business is transacted, in order to pick up information about current deals. The FBI is much more interested in the movement of large sums of dollars than it is in tax evasion, though the two often go hand in hand.

8. Scam-artist

A scam-artist is one who concocts a deal, totally without foundation, in order to find a real deal. He or she will offer to arrange finance from a bank which will not be revealed (ostensibly for the purpose of secrecy, but in fact because there is no bank) and in the course of discussion about the scam deal, will pick up information about real finance.

Normal scam ploys are: 'I can arrange a deal for one billion dollars if you can arrange collateral.' The other party then goes away and arranges the collateral and foolishly reveals his source. Suddenly the word is: 'Well the deal has gone up from one billion to five billion dollars.' This has the effect of destroying the deal because only one billion dollars of collateral has been arranged, so the scam-artist can legitimately say that the deal is off. But he is now in possession of the whereabouts of one billion dollars of collateral so at his next meeting he will state: 'I can arrange one billion dollars of collateral if you can provide the fund.' Sometimes it works, but more often than not, nowadays, dealers are aware of the ploy. Another term used for the same game is flim-flam.

9. Dixie

In the 1830s America was flooded by counterfeit money, making most bank notes suspect. The only nationally known notes to be reliable were those issued in Louisiana, bearing the name of the Citizen's Bank and Trust Company of New Orleans. The popular ten-dollar bill carried the French word 'Dix' on the back, so that Louisiana became famous as the 'land of Dixes' or 'Dixies' which meant solid currencies.

10. Dollar

The name dollar derived from its place of origin. In the sixteenth century silver coins were minted in a region of Bohemia called Joachimsthal and the coins were known as Joachimstaler, later shortened to

Thaler or dollar. The dollar sign – $ – is thought to be derived from Philip V of Spain's royal symbol – a ribbon winding between two pillars, the Pillars of Hercules; Gibraltar and Ceuta. The dollar became the official currency of the US in 1792.

11. Fees

The word fees derives from the old English word 'feoh' which means cattle. Cattle were bartered for other goods before money was developed.

12. Queer Street

The modern use of this phrase, meaning being in a state of near bankruptcy, derives from a custom adopted by English shopkeepers who would put a question mark or query next to the name of a customer whose credit was uncertain. The customer was said to be in 'Query' – later Queer Street – until he had paid his debts.

13. Blockers

In the highly strung world of sales, blockers are usually the secretaries or private assistants to decision-makers or buyers whom the salesman wishes to reach. There's not much selling can be done unless contact with the decision-maker can be made, so a 'blocker' is normally not well liked.

14. Nose-pickers

In the industries where salesmen front the production line the nose-picker is an individual who claims to have decision-making power but actually stands around wasting the salesman's time (picking their nose!).

15. The wanker

This character is someone with executive capacity who does not wish to make decisions because of lack of funds, uncertainty or a general dislike of salesmen. He or even she is probably the most unpopular person with the salesman because the target is there but cannot be achieved and therefore frustration is at its highest. Thus the rather vulgar term!

16.   Mr Prospect

Here is the one whom all salesmen aim to sit before, and to whom all manner of subtle and crude techniques will be demonstrated in order to win the sale. The means do not matter when Mr Prospect is available, only the end is important.

17.   The guinea

One pound and one shilling (or twenty-one shillings) is a guinea, used as a general currency up to 1914 when the sovereign also ceased to be a common measure of sterling. The name guinea derived from the gold brought back from the coast of Guinea towards the end of the seventeenth century.

18.   The florin

The florin took its name from Florence where florins were first struck.

19.   Big talkers

Big talkers are just that – they propose large transactions in order to impress real dealers in the hope that something will pass their way. The big talk never comes to anything, of course.

20.   Scalper

A term used in the Stock Exchange for one who buys very cheap so as to sell at less than the ruling price. A scalper is a sort of wholesale buyer who scalps the market and then sells off single units at below par.

21.   Flake

A flake is an individual who proposes financial trans-

actions which have no substance, either on the funding side or the collateral (security) side. They will more often than not put forward a fund for lending which they do not know for sure is real, hoping that something might come out of it. Because of the need for secrecy in the money market brokerage business it is easy for a flake to put forward a private funder or consortium without mentioning any specifics and people will believe him because the market is full of hopefuls. The transaction can reach as advanced a stage as a bank meeting to 'close' the deal and there is in fact no money to make the deal work. In this case the flake is likely to be carted off by the FBI or the Feds or CID for fraudulent dealing and perhaps prosecution by the bank for wasting its time.

22. The Grey Market

On one side there is the established money market – stock broking, banking etc. – the white market. On the other side there is the black market – laundering money, drug money, Mafia money, tax evasion etc. Somewhere in the middle, and overlapping on both sides, comes the grey market.

As the financial world becomes tighter and more restrictive, so the grey market grows. It includes arbitraging of money and metals, discounting of promissory notes, and movement of money through external and tax-haven accounts.

The banks are all involved in the grey market, for example when handling money and securities in external accounts: that is accounts outside the tax jurisdiction of the country, such as dollar accounts in England. The account may be opened in a corporate name or even just under a number, the transaction of money run through the account, payments made to individuals and corporations and in the space of one banking day, the whole matter closed and the papers shredded. The money is therefore never shown in the bank's balance sheets, and therefore not subject to the scrutiny of the Bank of England.

quotes about money

1. 'Let us all be happy and live within our means, even if we have to borrow the money to do it with.' Artemus Ward (1834–67).

2. 'Business, you know, may bring money, but friendship hardly ever does.' Jane Austen (1775–1817).

3. 'I'm tired of our taxing the poor people in our rich country and sending the money to rich people in poor countries.' Jimmy Carter 29 August 1976.

4. 'Nobody will persuade me there is no money about when I see so much spent on gambling, foreign travel, glossy magazines and plastic gnomes in every front garden.' Sir Frederick Seebohm, Barclays Bank Chairman, 1971.

5. 'There is no cure for the lack of a pay check but another pay check.' Joseph Curry, New York State Employment Service, 1971.

6. 'That's not too bad is it? At least not for him. It would be a life savings for me.' Albert Steward, Lord

Lambton's butler, regarding a £300 fine imposed on Lord Lambton for drug possession in 1973.

7. 'The requirements of a successful governor of the Bank of England are the tact and skill of an ambassador and the guile of a Romanian horse thief.' Harold Lever, 1974.

8. 'Money is not so important as a pat on the head.' Lord Snow, 1977.

9. 'There is no one, but no one, in this House who would do the job they're doing for a take-home pay of about £40 a week.' Denis Skinner MP on gravediggers, 1979.

10. 'If you see a Swiss banker jumping out of a window, jump after him – there's bound to be money in it.' Voltaire.

11. 'Money, it turned out, was exactly like sex, you thought of nothing else if you didn't have it and thought of other things if you did.' James Baldwin.

12. 'If you would know what the Lord God thinks of money, you have only to look at those to whom he gives it.' Maurice Baring.

13. 'To have money is to be virtuous, honest, beautiful and witty. And to be without it is to be ugly and boring and stupid and useless.' Jean Giraudoux – from the *Mad Woman of Chaillot*.

14. 'Go into the street, and give one man a lecture on morality, and another a shilling, and see which will respect you the most.' Samuel Johnson.

15. 'I finally know what distinguishes man from the other beasts: financial worries.' Jules Renard.

16. 'When money speaks, the truth keeps silent.' Russian proverb.

17. 'There was a time when a fool and his money were soon parted – but now it happens to everyone.' Adlai Stevenson.

18. 'Some men worship rank, some worship heroes, some worship power, some worship God, and over all these ideals they dispute – but they all worship money.' Mark Twain.

19. 'Put not your trust in money, but your money in trust.' Oliver Wendell Holmes Sr.

20. 'A bank is a place that will lend you money if you can prove that you don't need it.' Bob Hope.

people, places and things that you heard of in the world of money but never understood

1. Amortization

A fancy way of describing what at least fifty per cent of the average men in the street do each month! Amortization is reducing a loan by regular instalments of capital and interest; like repaying a mortgage or loan. The qualifying factor for the repayment to be amortization is that the interest *and* the capital are being repaid. If only the interest is paid along the way, and the capital at the end, then that is not amortization.

2. Asset stripping

If the price of a company on the open market is lower than the sum value of its assets, it can be profitable to buy that company and then sell off all its assets –

or strip them, and then liquidate the company. The price of the company could be lower than its asset value if, for example, it had had a bad year because of inflation or changes in export capability. In this case it might be forced to sell out because of demanding creditors and the buyer might buy purely on the basis of stripping out the assets.

3. Balance of payments

To any government this is a particularly sensitive issue. A country's balance of payments is an accounting of the transactions in goods, services and money with other countries and international organizations. There are two accounts, a current account and a capital account, and they must of course balance.

The current account is made up of 'visible' trading, or in the US 'merchandise trade' – imports and exports, and 'invisible' trading which means payments and receipts for services such as banking, tourism, shipping and insurance, plus any interest payments on loans. Thirdly there are private transfers which comprise payments from migrant workers and finally official transfers such as debt interest payments.

On the capital account there are six entries: firstly, long-term capital flows, i.e. investments; secondly, short-term 'autonomous' capital flow: these are quick movement money investments where 'hot money' is exchanged through currencies at rapid profits on very short turn around. Thirdly, the balance is affected by changes in foreign exchange reserves; fourthly, by borrowings from international funds such as the IMF or the EEC; fifthly, by foreign exchange borrowing or lending by the public sector; and the last is a balancing item to account for lags or inconsistencies in the year's accounts.

If there is a large deficit in the balance of payments accounts the lenders will ask for repayment or an increased rate of interest. Political changes and policy adjustments can be demanded by lenders such as the IMF. On a world-wide scale surpluses are always matched by deficits so that if the OPEC (oil-producing) countries enjoy a large surplus through high-priced oil sales, there will be a deficit in the rest of the world. It's a strange prospect but just as a small company has a balance sheet with plus and minus, so does the planet Earth. Theoretically world balance of payment statisticians should manage to create a perfect balance of nil, i.e. exact balance on either side, but in recent years this has not been possible, due perhaps to delays in the receipt of information. But at the moment the world suffers from a deficit balance of \$100 billion! If our space-travelling world buyer came to visit; we'd have to pay him to strip the planet's assets!

4. Bankruptcy

If a company goes bankrupt in the UK an official receiver, usually an accountant, is appointed by the courts to sell the company by assets and distribute the receipts to all those due to be paid. In the US the term used is 'Chapter 11 bankruptcy' where the courts receive a plan from the company to recover its situation over a specified period; the company is protected by the courts for that period from litigation by its creditors. In the States, if a company is near bankruptcy, just the threat of the words Chapter 11 is usually sufficient to shut up the creditors. Also in the UK, threaten bankruptcy and normally the creditors will back off and hope for recovery.

5. Certificate of deposit

Commonly known as CD's these papers were first

issued by America's largest bank, Citicorp, in 1961, and in Britain in 1968. They are fixed-term, interest-bearing deposits – i.e. you give your money to a bank and the bank gives you a CD with the term of the loan and the interest on the face of it. Once you have a CD you can sell it in the open market for an amount somewhere between its face value and its maturity value – so CDs are therefore used to raise loans. Generally they are provided by banks of large standing, only in relation to very large sums of money. You can't get a CD for your £5 piggy bank content. At time of writing there are approximately $160 billion worth of CDs around in the States and £9 billion in the UK.

6. The Dow Jones Index
The Dow Jones Index is the New York Stock Exchange barometer, the UK equivalent being the *Financial Times* Industrial Ordinary Share Index. The Dow Jones Index takes the share prices of thirty typical companies and measures their movements to give an overall market picture. There are also specialist Dow indices for transport shares utility shares and bonds.

7. Dutch auction
This could be called an upside-down auction, where the price of the goods starts at a deliberately inflated level and the bids are made against a reducing price – the first one to get nervous gets the goods too.

8. The Eurodollar
Very simply – US dollars placed in accounts outside the US.

9. The Fed
The Federal Reserve Bank is the US equivalent of the Bank of England – the United States central bank.

Feds are guys who work for the Federal Reserve Bank. The Fed is responsible for paper money distribution and coinage, for the management of the US monetary policy and the regulation of the US banking system. Unlike the Old Lady of Threadneedle Street, the Fed does not demand that all 14,000 US banks have to belong to the Federal Reserve System. Roughly 40 per cent of US banks do belong and these 40 per cent handle about 75 per cent of the US banking deposits.

As a matter of interest, during the latter quarter of 1983, when the financial brokerage market in London was so heavily involved in the business of arbitraging money (see p. 78) there were Federal and FBI agents posted in most of the City of London major branches to watch out for US tax dodgers and familiar flakes (see p. 82). The Fed watches, theoretically, every dollar that passes hands through every bank in the world. It is not possible to place more than $10,000 in a bank account in the US without the Fed or the IRS knowing about it. The Fed is very jealous of its dollars!

10. Fiscal drag

OK, this one needs a bit of a deep breath – Tax is levied in fixed bands according to income, and allowances are fixed according to the last budget. If pre-tax incomes rise while the tax bands and allowances stay the same, then tax payments increase too and people are shoved up into higher tax brackets through no fault of their own – simply because of inflationary effects. This means the government collects more revenue for the simple reason that its inefficiency and bad economic planning has caused people to appear to earn more! Get it? The net effect is that people don't care to increase their effort if all that is happening is that inflation is eating away at their money, forcing them into higher tax brackets and making them feel generally rotten! What a fiscal drag.

11. Gearing

Gearing is used in the loose-tongued world of finance in several different ways but basically it is a way of assessing the extent of a company's indebtedness. The formula used most often is the debt ratio, or another method – the debt/equity ratio. The higher the number the more trouble the company is in. Gearing can also be used, wrongly, to describe 100-per-cent-plus borrowings against assets or cash expectations. In the 60s and early 70s era of rapid property-value increases individuals and companies often borrowed against the potential value of a property, taking sometimes as much as 300 per cent of the purchase value of the property on the expectation of value increases. This was called gearing, or over-gearing. Many bankruptcies came about at the end of the property boom when prices slid back down, leaving geared loans hanging in mid-Queer Street.

12. Gilt-edged stocks

Gilt has nothing to do with gold or guilt, needless to say (you'd be surprised what people think!) but is supposedly a safe investment bet. Gilts are any government security except Treasury Bills, and are sold according to whatever the government is looking for in the way of money from the open market. Originally gilts were floated on, say, a fifteen-year investment basis to raise money from the public sector, to be repaid at the end of the period, with interest or dividend payable each half-year or annually. In fact, it's all a complete fallacy because as soon as one gilt is repaid another will be floated – perpetual borrowing against the substance of the United Kingdom government, which is apt to change every four years and puts up around £11 billion in currency against about £4 billion worth of gold. This, in itself, illustrates the total fantasy of the basis of money in modern society – it's all a complete hoax!

Nevertheless, if you're playing the game, as we all must, gilts are a good bet and may be bought at various discounts and various interest rates which are fixed according to a daily level printed in the *Financial Times* and according to how much your broker can beat down the price from the existing stockholders.

Gilts are also occasionally used for bulk purchase on larger scales where a trustee of funds is looking to make a 'turn' on the money. He will take on 100 per cent of the fund and buy the gilts at say 89 per cent of face value, pocketing the balance of 11 per cent. The gilt will pay interest at the quoted level and repay 100 per cent of the capital at the end of the term, so no one has lost, and everyone has gained because the government will probably lend on the money at a higher rate, or invest it in roads or housing to the benefit of taxpayers.

13. Hot money
Hot money, said to burn bankers' fingers, is cash held in a particular currency which may be required to change into another currency at a moment's notice. The fast selling is due to the owners of the money chasing the highest interest rates which can alter suddenly, and if the amount of hot money changing currencies reaches high levels it can change the currency rates down without warning and thus cause ripples throughout the world.

14. Interbank rate
Banks have a habit of lending to each other, usually for short periods of time, sometimes even overnight.

In each financial capital there is a thing called the overnight money market which literally means the price of lending money between banks for a twenty-four hour period or less. In the London interbank market or the Libor market, the rate runs around 11 per cent at time of writing.

15. The International Monetary Fund – IMF

This is a sort of money club, with some 140 member countries, each contributing a quota to the IMF, determined by the size of the country (and other considerations). The USA provides 20.8 per cent of the quotas, Germany 5.3 per cent, Japan 4.1 per cent, UK 7.2 per cent. The quotas are paid partly in the national currency and partly in foreign, mostly dollars, or gold. This means that a great deal of the money in the IMF funds is unlendable because it is made up of currencies that aren't worth anything.

Members can withdraw amounts as loans at will up to certain limits, without problems. Over these limits it gets tougher and the IMF can make policy change demands on the borrowers before making the loan. The maximum a country can borrow is $4^1/_2$ times its quota.

16. John Maynard Keynes (1883–1946)

One of the most influential economists of history, his most famous work published in 1936 was 'General Theory of Employment Interest and Money' which sounds horrendously boring and is, but it changed the entire emphasis of central government thinking away from 'microeconomics' to 'macroeconomics' – i.e. that economies could be balanced at less than full capacity employment, so that it was on the government's back to ensure enough effective demand to produce full employment. The effect of his work was incredible and governments everywhere took on the full responsibility of providing the energy for full employment. Apart from his writing Keynes was an adviser to the British Treasury and a director of the Bank of England, editor of *The Economist* and bursar of King's College, Cambridge. As if that wasn't enough he was also a director of several City institutions and a member of the Bloomsbury Group.

17. Lloyds

Not the bank but the insurance. Lloyds started when Edward Lloyd opened a coffee shop in Lime Street, London in 1688 and ever since the company has been the world's leading and most eccentric insurance system. On the outside there are a bunch of 16,000 people or 'names' in the business, who provide backing and money to fulfil insurance risks taken, on their behalf, by members of Lloyds. These members are in groups and they compete against one another for the business. The 'names' are liable for the risks taken on by the members without limitation so that it could theoretically happen that they would lose everything, though in practice they are rarely asked to contribute a penny. In return for their backing they receive a share of the profits of the insurance premiums earned.

Scandals in the Lloyds syndicates occurred in the early 1980s when members were found to be channelling portions of the insurance premiums to external re-insurers in which they, the members, had an undeclared interest – allegedly, of course. The Lloyds self-policing methods are soon to come more strictly under the wing of the Department of Trade in order to prevent such scandals occurring again.

18. Nobel Prize

The Nobel Prize is an annual economics prize awarded by Sweden's Central Bank and not by the

Nobel Foundation. The winner is, however, regarded as a Nobel laureate.

19. Overnight money

The overnight lending market is the shortest-term lending market and consists of one bank with an excess of deposit money lending it to another bank with a shortage for that day. It is therefore basically a method of banks balancing their daily business,

using each other as props. Overnight rates can grow to astronomical heights on some occasions – even as much as 50 per cent (per annum).

20. Retail Price Index

In the UK, this is the most normal way of measuring the rate of inflation, i.e. how fast money is becoming worth less or more – normally less! In the US and most European countries the equivalent is the Consumer Price Index, which shows prices of a fixed number of goods, services etc., according to the spending habits of a typical family. Each of the items on the list is given a 'weight' or number, such as food which is weighted at 20.6 per cent and fuel at 6.2 per cent. Because of the variations on the term 'typical' – i.e. there is no such thing as a typical family, the indexation is varied – for pensioners say, or for different areas of the country. It's not what you'd call a perfect measure but it's the only one we have.

21. Sinking fund

This is a way of paying off a loan at the end of its term by saving money along the way and taking advantage of the increase by interest of the saved money so that effectively less is paid at the maturity of the loan than if a chunk of money is simply paid at maturity. A common way of arranging such funds is through an insurance-backed monthly or annual scheme which reduces the tax liability on the savings and increases at a very high rate of interest. Pensions are also sometimes used as sinking funds – if the term can be reconciled with retirement age.

22. Adam Smith

Adam Smith is regarded as the forefather of economic thought. His book *Inquiry into the Nature and Causes of the Wealth of Nations* (1776) is still considered as the bible of classical economics. His writing emphasized the importance of specialization, technical progress and investment as the main methods of economic increase. Above all he regarded free enterprise or self-interest to be the mainstay of progress and the basis for national benefit.

23. Soft loans

These are loans made for semi-philanthropic motives, i.e. with interest charged at much lower rates than the commercial market will normally allow. A government might give a soft loan to an industrial concern which they are eager to see successful and in some cases Arab lenders will advance money for very low rates of interest in order to deploy their excess capital to the best effect in worthy causes such as hospital building and generally in areas where the world will benefit.

24. Tax havens

These are areas of the world where the local authorities attract trade by offering very low tax rates to people or corporations who wish to divert income away from the major tax areas such as the UK and the US. It is very hard for any individual or corporation to exist in the US or the UK for long without paying full tax there. It is becoming, however, increasingly hard actually to find parts of the world where it is possible to 'hide' income from the tax authorities because of the unwillingness of the tax-haven areas to become irresponsible about monies passing through their hands. The most commonly used tax havens at the time of writing (and they are changing all the time) are Monaco, Jersey, the Bahamas, Liechtenstein, the Cayman Islands, Nasau, Luxembourg, Hong Kong and Cyprus.

25. Venture capital
Certain financial organizations like merchant banks, pension funds and groups of wealthy individuals will provide capital for start-up or new ventures in which there is a high risk to the investment. Normally the funder will wish to take a share of the corporation to whom the money is lent as well as perhaps an interest payment or a lump sum payment if the company goes public.

26. Wall Street
New York's financial centre, running one third of a mile up from Lower Manhattan Island, New York. In Wall Street, most of the buildings are very tall, specially built to house punters who may wish to follow Swiss bankers after a market crash! However, in Manhattan it is now very difficult to get the windows open due to the predominance of air conditioning. The New York Stock Exchange is on Wall Street as well as the US Stock Exchange.

27. The World Bank
The International Bank for Reconstruction and Development (IBRD) was established in 1944 at the

Bretton Woods conference for the purpose of financing post-war Europe's reconstruction. It has now become the world's largest provider of development aid to poor countries.

The head office of the bank is in Washington DC.

25

money proverbs

A list of 25 sayings to live by – or not, depending on how you feel about money.

Proverbs are described in the *Oxford Dictionary* as 'short well-known sayings stating a general truth' – in other words you believe them if they suit you, and if they don't, it don't matter. Needless to say proverbs about money are numerous – it is after all a subject of some fascination to at least 99.9 per cent of the world. As an amateur philosopher the author would like to set this particular ball in motion by coining (!) a new proverb, trusting that it will go down in the annals of history for as long as the rest on this list:

1. Money doesn't exist. (Think about it.)

2. A beggar can never be bankrupt. (And probably wouldn't care if he was.)

3. A horn spoon holds no poison. (The idea is that if a fellow can't afford anything better than a horn spoon he ain't worth poisoning.)

4. The beggar may sing before the thief. (This may not be entirely true in New York City at 3.00 a.m. around 8th Avenue and 42nd Street – there it is said a mugger will take the beard off your face, and if you have the nerve to sing at him, probably one or two other vital bits as well.)

5. Poverty is an enemy of good manners. (The implication being that those who have no money slobber when they eat!)

6. Need makes the naked man run. (Especially on a winter's day in Glasgow.)

7. An empty purse fills the face with wrinkles. (Largely because of squinting the eyes to see into the bottom of it.)

8. The devil dances in an empty pocket. (Which is why tramps are often seen to be scratching their inner leg.)

9. An empty sack cannot stand upright. (Huh–hum.)

10. Poverty is the worst guard for chastity. (Or – if you're poor you have more fun.)

11. It is better to be a beggar than a fool. (The real problems begin when you're both – but it's all right to be rich and stupid.)

12. The rich man thinks of the future, the poor man thinks of today. (This is a Chinese proverb, but is echoed in the Eastern philosophies – if you're penniless you concentrate on the moment – living hand to mouth – and thus become more aware of your spiritual being. If you're rich you're constantly planning what you can do with it. It's not true, of course – as one day I plan to prove!)

13. He that is needy when he is married, shall be rich when he is buried. (A 1980s version of this might be: He that is needy when he is married shall be almost rich when he has his first coronary.)

14. Riches have wings. (Chance would be a fine thing.)

15. Money is the root of all evil. (This is in fact a mis-quote from the Bible, 1 Timothy 6:10 – the real version is: The love of money is the root of all evil.)

16. Set a beggar on horseback and he'll ride to the devil. (Witness some recent football pools winners.)

17. Avarice hoards itself poor, charity gives itself rich.

18. Little good comes of gathering.

19. Poverty wants many things, and avarice all.

20. Avarice is the only passion that never ages.

21. The older the bird the more unwillingly it parts with its feathers. (I know a few old birds like that!)

22. Moderation in all things.

23. Do not all you can; spend not all you have; believe not all you hear; and tell not all you know. (This proverb should be the author's standby.)

24. Enough is as good as a feast.

25. Discontent is the first step in progress.

names for money in the English language

Blunt	Dimnock	Sand
Brass	The Doins	Slippery stuff
Cabbage	Dumps	Spoons
Chink	Flour	Suds
Chips	Gingerbread	Tin
Dibs	Groceries	Velvet
Dinero	Juice	Bangers
Do-re-mi	Mammon	The hard
Dough	Mint sauce	Iron
Filthy lucre	Necessary evil	Greenbacks
Gelt	Nourishment	Jack
Spinach	for the bank	Kale
Bullets	account	Legal tender
Bacon	Ointment	Lettuce
Bunce	Pay dirt	Long green
Coal	Pieces	Loot
Crap	Powder	Lucre
Born in Egypt	Rubbish	Mazuma

Moolah
Mopus
Needful
Ammunition
Bees and
    Honey
Checks
Coconuts
Coin
Courage
Dingbats
Dots
The Evil
Frozen Work
Glue
Honey
Junk
Manna
Mon
Nonsense
Oof
Pazaza
Pitch
Pot of Honey
Root of all evil
Sauce
Smuties
Spuds
Sugar and
    honey
Tomatoes
Wad
Brads
Hardware
Ironman
Ooftish

Pelt
Rhino
Readies
Rocks
Scratch
Shekels
Smash
Stuff
Stumpy
Sugar
Swag
Wampum
Lump
Ballast
Berries
Cherries
Coin of the
    realm
Collateral
Cush
Dirt
The doubloons
Fat
Geetus
Grease
Horse nails
Kopecks
Mica
Moss
Nuggets
Oil
Oughday
Plush
Pony
Remedy
Salt

Scads
Snow
Stamps
Syrup
Toot
Buttons
Heigh ho silver
Junglers
Specic
Beans
Gravy
Roll
Bucks
Ducats
Pesos
Chickenfeed
Peanuts
Lolly
Spondulicks
Simoleans
Boodle
Browns
Clink
Collat
Corn
Dimes
Do-di-o-do
Dues
Fish
Gilt
Grip
Jake
Liquid assets
Mint drops
Muck
Oday

Oil of palms
Paint
Possibles
Potatoes
Rowdy
Salve
Shells
Soap
Stiff

That thing
Trash
Whackers
Charms
Holystones
Joyberries
Metal
Pewter

Readies
Silverware
Ridge
Shiners
Washers
Nails
Rivets
Shiny

names for the US dollar

Almighty dollar
Buckerod
Dollo
Bob
Cabbage
Ducat
Boffo
Case
Fish
Rubbish dollar

Buck
Dobe
Kopeck
Oner
Peso
Pig
Onespot
Piaster
Potato

Scream and
hollar
Seminole
Shekel
Simolean
Single
Spot
Tomato
Baloney dollar

names for the US silver dollar

Ball	Iron man	Plate
Can	Thumbnail	Platter
Clanker	Berry	Plug
Smackarod	Chip	Plunk
Banger	Iron smacker	Plunker
Cartwheel	Wacker	Rock
Coachwheel	Biscuit	Rocker
Smackola	Clam	Seed
Bat	Medal	Shiner
Check	Wheel	Sinker
Drum	Bone	Slug
Stone	Clank	Smack
Bean	Plank	Smacker
Checker	Planker	Smackarino

names for the US dollar bill

Alf	Jew/Jewish flag	Green
Greenback	Case note	Greeny
Greenboy	Lamb's tongue	Martha Washington
Green jacket	Frogskin	
Bathide	Grenie	Mint leaf
Greener	Leaf	Plaster

Pussy rag	Skin	Washington
Rag	Toadskin	

foreign countries' names for money

1.	France	L'Argent, monnaie, especes
2.	Germany	Geld
3.	Holland	Geld
4.	Italy	Moneta, denaro, soldi
5.	Serbia	Novac
6.	Czechoslovakia	Penize
7.	Spain	Dinero, papel moneda
8.	Portugal	Dinheiro, moeda, sistema, monetaria
9.	Sweden	Pengar
10.	Denmark	Penge, mønt
11.	Iceland	Peningar, mønnid
12.	Russia	Moheta, cepeopo
13.	Poland	Moneta, pieniadze
14.	Slovene	Denar
15.	Albania	Te holla, monedhe
16.	Lithuania	Pinigas
17.	Slovak	Peniaze
18.	Somalia	La'ag
19.	Housa	Kurdi
20.	Turkey	Para, nakit, servet
21.	Hungary	Penz
22.	Swahili	Fedha

23.	Indonesia	Uang
24.	Malaya	Wang
25.	Samoa	Tupe
26.	Tonga	Pa'anga, silini
27.	Fiji	i lavo
28.	Hawaii	Kala
29.	Pihto	Moni
30.	Sotho	Chelete, mali
31.	Estonia	Raha
32.	Malta	Flus, gid, ghana

Section Four

BAD MONEY

Bad money keeps you awake at night, in conscience and fear of apprehension. Those who say it does not are lying, but the world is full of those resigned to sleepless nights, for in their way they are always sleeping.

16

ways in which crime made money

1. One of the weirdest ways money has been conned out of an innocent, gullible public is through mail-order fraud. Mail-order fraud brought in $514 million in 1982 for the crafty conmen of the business even though there were 17,650 convictions. The most bizarre example of this type of fraud occurred in 1946 when there were rumours everywhere that Adolf Hitler was still alive and a semi-literate miner from Middlesboro, Kentucky, called William H. Johnson, dreamed up the idea of pretending to be Hitler through the US mail. Johnson wrote to numerous suckers all over the United States, pretending to be Hitler and writing of his plans to take over America, always adding lines requesting money and receiving it in large quantities. He collected a total of $15,000 and only ended up in the hands of the police because of the death of one of his most successful suckers. Promising high-powered positions to those he corresponded with, he would add such niceties as 'please send money and shoes. I was unable to go to an important meeting because I had no shoes.' Even though Johnson's prose was almost totally illiterate, the recipients of the letters were happy to fulfil his requests.

2. Probably the most famous conman of all time was Joseph 'Yellow Kid' Weil, who for eight years retained the title of dean of American confidence men. He started his dazzling career as a boy in his father's saloon selling Meriweather's Elixir to farmers as a cure-all for every conceivable ailment. The nickname Yellow Kid derived from a comic strip to which he was addicted, 'Hogan's Alley' in which his favourite character, the Yellow Kid, was illustrated as a lovable conman.

Weil went into partnership with a plain-clothed cop named Fred 'The Deacon' Buckminster, working on the vice squad, who arrested Weil in 1908: Weil had contracted to paint City Hall with a waterproof paint – which washed off with the first drop of rain.

Weil is said to have produced a wad of bills from his pocket on their way to the police station – placing it in Buckminster's hands. There was more than $10,000 in the wad and the cop was astonished enough to take off his shield and pocket it with the money – becoming thereafter Weil's partner in crime.

An example of their scams occurred when the two conmen rented an abandoned bank in Indiana, filled it with conmen who pretended to be wealthy investors, and fooled passers-by into depositing their money in the sham bank.

On another occasion they dressed up as US Army officers, contracted with farmers to buy horses for the government, and paid off the ranchers with fake, official-looking cheques.

The Yellow Kid, by his own estimate during his hundredth year, reckoned to have conned over $12 million from suckers during his lifetime. But he died broke and was buried in an unmarked grave near Chicago.

3. During the Second World War $20,000,000 (worth around $200 million today) was stolen by members of the American and German armies from various parts of Europe. None of this wealth was ever recovered and none of the perpetrators have ever been brought to trial. These notes can still be acquired on the collectors' market for about £15 each.

4. During the civil war in Lebanon in January 1976 a force of guerilla soldiers blew the vaults of the British Bank of the Middle East and cleared the bank of approximately $50 million.

5. Between 1964 and 1973 64,000 faked insurance policies were created on computer at the Equity Funding Corporation in the US. The total amount paid out in computer cheques was $2000 million.

6. Philip II of Spain offered a reward of $1,000,000 for anyone who succeeded in assassinating William of Orange in the late sixteenth century. The man who succeeded in killing the king, Balthazar Gerard, really earned his money – even though he didn't actually get paid. After shooting William he was taken to the torture chambers where his joints were dislocated and his body scarred with flame. He was then taken to the scaffold where, before a large crowd, his right hand was burned off, red hot pincers were applied to tear off his flesh and his abdomen was slit open and the contents drawn out. His legs and arms were then chopped off close to the trunk. During this entire horrifying procedure Gerard did not utter a single groan, nor display any emotional response and remained fully conscious and alive until his heart was cut out and slung in his face! Finally the head was severed from what remained of the body

7. Jack Gilbert Graham of Colorado had spent much of his adult life claiming fraudulently on insurance policies. He blew up his own service station, placed his car on a railway track, and claimed. Finally, by 1955 he had rid himself of almost everything for insurance claims – except his mother!

He had taken out a $37,500 insurance policy and also stood to inherit $150,000 on her death. So he loaded up her briefcase with dynamite and put her aboard a flight on United Airlines. Forty-four people were killed when it exploded. He was electrocuted in 1957.

8. Richard I of England, returning from the Third Crusade, was kidnapped by Duke Leopold of Austria in 1192. Emperor Henry VI, who had put Duke Leopold up to the kidnapping, demanded a ransom of £150,000 or about £10 million now. England's throne was then unoccupied, so Richard's brother John delayed the ransom payment and in the meantime hopped on to the empty throne. The merchant class in England were so much more afraid of what John would do to them if he stayed on the throne, that they raised the money themselves and paid Leopold and the Emperor, who released Richard at once.

9. In 1532 the ruthless conqueror Francisco Pizarro travelled to Peru in search of riches. The Inca ruler Atahualpa visited him in his fortress, bringing several hundred Incas along with him. Pizarro's soldiers killed the Incas and held Atahualpa captive, telling his people that they must provide a fortune in gold for his return. The Incas filled a hall twenty-two feet long, seventeen feet wide and seven feet high with gold, and another hall twice as large with silver. It took them almost five months to complete the ransom request. The modern-day value of such a haul would be around $175 million. Pizarro took the silver and gold and then killed the Inca ruler in 1533.

10. In December 1927 twelve-year-old Marian Parker, daughter of successful lawyer Perry Parker, was kidnapped by William Hickman who demanded a ransom of $7500. Parker met with Hickman on a lonely road and paid the money. Hickman threw Parker's daughter down wrapped in a blanket, and to Parker's horror, once Hickman had driven away, he found his daughter strangled and with her legs cut off. Hickman was caught and hanged at San Quentin in 1928.

11. In December 1968 Barbara Jane Mackle, daughter of a wealthy building contractor, Robert Mackle of Florida (a friend of President Nixon), was roused from sleep in her university residence in Atlanta by a kidnapper who chloroformed her and took her in his car. Barbara, twenty years old, was placed in a crude capsule, photographed with a sign in her hands reading 'Kidnapped', and buried alive. The kidnappers gave her food and water and made provisions for light and air, leaving elaborate instructions inside the capsule for the girl to follow, saying that they were staying in a house nearby and that they would check on her every few hours until her father paid the $500,000 ransom, when she would be released. The photo and the ransom demand were sent to Robert Mackle who quickly produced the money. Agents sent to meet with the kidnappers and deliver the money frightened them off but on 20 December, three days after the burial, a call was received at the FBI offices in Atlanta, directing the agents to the site where Barbara was buried. They went immediately to the site and dug her out furiously, opening the capsule to find the young girl staring up at them after eighty-three hours buried alive. All she had to say was, 'You're the handsomest men I've ever seen.' The culprits were caught and imprisoned, the man for life and the woman for seven years.

12. At the end of the Second World War, after the German surrender, a lorry loaded with £21 million in 'white' five-pound notes was handed over to US counter-espionage agents. A Bank of England official travelled to Germany to investigate one of the biggest frauds in the history of the world, a fraud which was created to destroy the British economy, and almost succeeded.

The plan was the brain child of Gestapo chief Himmler and began two years before the end of the war when batches of £100,000 began to appear in major cities around Europe. The notes were near-perfect forgeries but no lead was available to the British authorities until the truck was picked up in 1945.

The civil servants in Germany had refused to be part of the forgery so that engravers and printers were recruited from the concentration camps, promised special treatment and put to work in a special camp near Berlin. Reproducing the paper used by the Bank of England was one of the most difficult tasks, and then printing the correct serial numbers, but once these problems had been solved the first batch of notes was presented to Gestapo agents in neutral countries who had no problem spending the money or changing it in foreign banks.

When the war ended Himmler ordered the plan to be stopped but the foremost engineer of the work, Major Bernhard Kruger, persuaded him to allow the forgery to continue in a hideout in the Alps so that escaping German officers could be supplied with ready money. The Allies, however, closed in and destroyed the plates. The forgers were attempting to bury the £21 million from the truck when they were stopped by agents. Bank of England officials later estimated that nine million notes with a face value of £140 million were produced during the period. For a while the notes continued to turn up on the black market but Major Kruger was never found.

13. One of the great salesmen of criminal history was a Scotsman named Arthur Ferguson who hit upon the idea of spoofing American tourists into buying various of the world's great national monuments. He would stand in Trafalgar Square in London and approach rich-looking tourists, confidentially explaining that the British government was in such a severe state of penury that it was willing to consider the sale of such major items as Nelson's Column (including the lions), Big Ben and Buckingham Palace.

Ferguson talked several unsuspecting (and presumably very gullible) Americans into paying £6000 for Trafalgar Square's famous monument prior to delivery! £1000 was paid for Big Ben and £2000 put down as a deposit on Buckingham Palace.

Ferguson then decided he should extend his activities to the country where the action really was. In 1925 he arrived in Washington and promptly sold a ninety-nine-year lease on the White House to an American rancher for $100,000 a year, with the first year's payment in advance. His fortune now secured, this wily Scotsman could have retired but his ego got the better of him in an attempt to sell off the Statue of Liberty. New York Harbour had to be widened, he told an unsuspecting Australian, and the statue was in the way. But his victim did not have the $100,000 deposit readily available so had to make several visits to banks and credit establishments to collect his resources together. Ferguson stuck to his man like glue and during their walk about New York the tourist took a photograph of Ferguson in front of the statue herself. After several days' work the Australian became suspicious as Ferguson pushed him harder and harder and eventually took the picture to the police – the chance they had been waiting for.

Ferguson was arrested and imprisoned for five years, but upon completion of his sentence in 1930 he moved to Los Angeles where he lived in luxury – paid for by a string of new confidence tricks – until his death in 1938.

14. In 1911 six Americans each paid $300,000 for the *Mona Lisa* painting, all six paintings being the work of one Yves Chaudron, a brilliant master forger.

The proud owners believed they possessed the real thing because the *Mona Lisa* had been stolen from the Louvre that year. The method used to establish the authenticity of the fakes was very simple: the original was framed with a fake sealed into the frame behind it. The buyer was told to examine the painting and then mark the back of it with his own mark. Then when the picture was secretly delivered the buyer could be sure of its authenticity. The fake with the mark on it back would then be delivered.

However the culprits never made any money directly out of the original as one of their party stole it from them and was reported by a Florentine art dealer to whom he attempted to sell it.

15. The Louvre in Paris bought and exhibited a priceless gold tiara, paying 200,000 francs for the

Money Lisa

piece, about £90,000 in modern values. The tiara, reported to have been found in Olbia, an ancient site in southern Russia, remained on show for seven years. The piece was inscribed in Greek with the words 'The Senate and People of Olbia to the Great Invincible Saitaphernes'.

The tiara was in a remarkable state of preservation considering its age, about 2200 years, which was not really surprising as it was actually only a few months old.

The true story of its origin, which emerged seven years later, was that in 1895 a Rumanian wheat dealer named Schapschelle Hochmann had commissioned a goldsmith named Israel Rouchomovsky to make a gold tiara in antique style, and paid 2000 roubles – about £3500 – for the job. He then systematically battered the piece to give it the appearance of age and sold it to the Louvre.

The piece would still be on display today had it not been for a French painter, known as Elina, falsely claiming to have made the tiara, thus exposing the fraud. The Louvre still occasionally displays the piece in exhibitions of fakes.

16. Adam Worth, a Londoner living in the mid-nineteenth century, had selective tastes in art – though none of the wealth to acquire it. Rather than deprive himself of his greatest love, he simply stole great works. His best-documented theft was that of Gainsborough's *The Duchess of Devonshire* which Worth burgled from Agnew & Agnew in 1878. He offered to return the masterpiece if the authorities would release a friend of his from jail, but the fellow got out anyway on a legal technicality, so Worth decided to keep the painting after all. For years, until 1901, he argued with Agnew & Agnew about returning the picture, continually changing his mind. Finally, the art gallery agreed to pay him a very large but unfortunately undisclosed sum and the painting was returned. A few days later Worth died of tuberculosis and so got little benefit from his profitable acquisition, other than being able to look at it for twenty-three years!

less obvious ways in which crime paid

1. The international drug trade is now a vast, high-earning business, with profits of between £23,000 million to £36,000 million a year. In 1981 there was a bumper opium crop in Thailand, Laos, Pakistan and Burma and an estimated 400-plus tons of heroin were grown throughout the world. The increase in value of such drugs from the original purchase to the street pusher is between fifteen and twenty times. In countries like Bolivia the sale of drugs is a vital part of the national economy. In Colombia the largest export used to be coffee, at around £750 million a year, but now marijuana and cocaine account for £2,500 million a year.

2. In Miami, Florida there exists an underground economy of drug smuggling and money laundering which produces around $40 billion a year. Law enforcement officials estimate that in 1981 between $7 and $10 billion was made from drug trafficking in that area alone.

3. The money laundering that occurs in Florida is the other major method by which individuals make their fortunes without paying tax on the income. Cash is carried in large cases into the Miami banks where it is 'cleaned', i.e. changed into other bills or used to buy municipal bonds and other forms of tax-exempt holdings with few reporting requirements. The cash acquired from drug trafficking is laundered in this way so that the original money is untraceable.

4. In the banking world, a recent game was played with bank confirmation of a draft. A forged bank draft was presented to an American bank for cashing. The draft was for 100 million US dollars and the presenter had opened an account which would subsequently transfer the money elsewhere. The banker naturally wished to call the bank on which the draft was drawn to verify the funds. Meanwhile, outside the other bank, who had not, of course, given out the forged draft, there was a man underground who tapped into the telephone lines to the bank, ready to receive the enquiry call. Once he heard the correct identification codes from the bank where the draft was deposited, he broke into the call and answered as if he were the banker at that end, verified the draft and hung up.

5. Bribery is another common method of earning, though in many parts of the world it is not regarded as a crime – merely a method of oiling the wheels of industry! In Nigeria, native entrepreneurs offer their

Itchy palms

expert knowledge in helping foreign investments through the many layers of bureaucracy. In return for this inside ability bribes are piled high and a foreign invester will add to an investment programme of say £50 million, a further £5 million for the services of these native partners. In Mexico one of the most popular methods of moving a deal through quickly is by the use of £60-per-night call girls.

The cost of war

War has been going on in one part of the world or another almost continuously since man first called himself civilized. In our own, recent history, war has certainly been continuous since 1939. Because, in general terms, we prefer to forget or ignore this state of existence, the monies spent on the activities of war are only lightly published.

So this is the war account book for *The Book of Money Lists*.

1. The total costs of the most recent wars.

The Falklands crisis cost, in terms accountable to the British taxpayer, £700,000,000 ($1,225,000,000).

The Vietnam War, according to estimates published by the *Daily Telegraph* on 30 April 1975 in the UK, cost the US taxpayer $138,974,000,000 (£79,413,000,000).

A certain Mr Adolf Hitler, in exercising his ambitions, ended up costing the world rather more than both these two wars and most other wars in history all put together. According to estimates published by *The World Almanac* in 1950 the following were the military and property costs of the Second World War:

Military costs:
US	$330,030,463,080
UK	£100,000,000,000
USSR	$192,000,000,000

Germany	$272,900,000,000
Italy	$ 94,000,000,000
Japan	$ 56,000,000,000
TOTAL	$1,064,930,463,084

Property damage came to a total of $230,900,000,000.

2. Some modern comparisons:

In 1981 the world spent $520 billion dollars on the military – that's just half of the cost of the Second World War in one year. NATO and the Warsaw Pact countries spent 70 per cent of this.

During 1978 the US spent $499 per head on its military requirements and the USSR $394 per head.

The cost of one Sea Harrier jet: £6 million
The cost of one 1942 Spitfire jet: approximately £5000.

The cost of one Sea Dart missile: £60,000
The cost of one Second World War V2 missile: approximately £3000.

The cost of one Type 42 destroyer: £150 million.
The cost of one Second World War destroyer: £400,000.

Section Five

PAY DAY

Once upon a time pay day was always on a Friday. With the advent of the computer payroll, pay day seems to be a moving feast – the eighth working day of the month, the sixteenth Friday after Lent, fourteen mega-hours before Wednesday after half-day closing. It is all probably part of the inter-national corporate scheme to confuse employees sufficiently that they cannot work out what they earn. Then the management, instead of giving pay increases, will give simplified pay days, so that we can all sleep better, knowing that we do actually earn something, sometimes, though never on a Friday.

15

recent political figures and their incomes

1. Australia	Malcolm Fraser	A$104,348	£61,315
2. Belgium	Senators	Bf900,000	£14,040
3. Canada	Pierre Trudeau	C$64,000	£28,000
4. China	P.M. Ziyang	Y 6,720	£1992
5. France	Francois Mitterrand	F511,200	£46,800
6. Germany	Chancellor Schmidt	Dm280,000	£65,520
7. India	P.M. Ghandhi	R27,000	£1560
8. Italy	President Pertini	L602 m	£250,460
9. Japan	P.M. Suzuki	Y20 m	£48,122
10. New Zealand	P.M. Muldoon	NZ$70,516	£30,564
11. South Africa	P.M. Botha	R63,000	£34,398
12. Sri Lanka	President Jayawardene	R6000	£127
13. Sweden	Each gov. seat	K115,000	£10,764
14. UK	Maggie Thatcher		£36,725
15. USA	President Reagan	$290,000	£150,800

different armed forces and their incomes

1. United States of America

General:	$62,500 p.a.	(£44,600)	Currency
Major:	$30,000 p.a.	(£21,640)	conversion
Sergeant:	$16,200 p.a.	(£11,570)	at Dls 1.4 to
Private:	$ 9400 p.a.	(£ 6700)	the pound.

2. United Kingdom

General	£42,750 p.a.
Major:	£15,830 p.a.
Sergeant:	£ 9439 p.a.
Private:	£ 6976 p.a.

3. Australia

General:	A$52,000	(£30,555)
Major:	A$26,500	(£15,570)
Sergeant:	Not available	
Private:	A$14,300	(£ 8400)

4. Portugal

General:	Esc 373,712	(£ 2976)
Major:	Esc 322,778	(£ 2570)
Sergeant:	Esc 177,224	(£ 1411)
Private:	Esc (18,937)	(£ 151)

5. West Germany

General:	Dm 114,686	(£28,836)
Major:	Dm 34,892	(£ 8164)
Sergeant:	Dm 24,271	(£ 5679)
Private:	Dm 15,249	(£ 3558)

6

different executives and their incomes

1. In 1977 Giovanni Agnelli, the chairman of Fiat, declared an income of 258 million lire or £107,328 from his position.

2. In 1978 Henry Ford declared an income of $1,056,000 or £549,120 from his position as chairman of the Ford Motor Company.

3. In 1979 Sir David Steel as chairman of British Petroleum declared an income of £120,385.

4. In 1980 Robert O. Anderson, chairman of Atlantic Richfield, a large oil company, declared an income of $1,650,000 or £858,000.

5. In 1979 Taisho Seiyaku, a Japanese pharmaceutical company, paid their chairman a staggering figure of 2 billion yen or £4.78 million.

6. In 1980 the chief executive of Deutsche Bank in West Germany earned Dm 796,000 or £186,300.

Annual income of

different teachers

1.	Abu Dhabi	$11,197	£ 5822
2.	Australia	$18,862	£ 9808
3.	Brazil	$ 4850	£ 2522
4.	Denmark	$21,856	£11,365
5.	West Germany	$22,395	£11,645
6.	Japan	$20,050	£10,426
7.	Switzerland	$36,526	£18,994
8.	United States	$22,455	£11,677
9.	United Kingdom	$13,530	£ 7035
10.	Thailand	$ 1976	£ 1027

Annual income of

different judges

1. In the United States of America a judge of the Supreme Court earns $81,300, or £42,300 a year. The Chief Justice, Mr Warren Burger, earns $84,700 or £44,000 a year.

2. In the United Kingdom Lord Denning, when Master of the Rolls and Lord of Appeal, received

£41,000 per annum as do the seventeen other Lords of Appeal.

3. In West Germany judges of the High Court earn approximately Dm 143,611 or £33,605 per annum.

4. In Australia a chief justice earns A$91,400 or £53,700.

10

different bus drivers and their incomes

1.	Amsterdam	£12,200
2.	Athens	£4400
3.	Colombia	£1200
4.	West Germany	£13,360
5.	England (London)	£7200
6.	Luxembourg	£14,250
7.	Manila	£1100
8.	New York	£15,110
9.	Paris	£9310
10.	Zurich	£17,125

Motto – if you want to drive buses – go to Switzerland!

The pay of the world's top sportspeople

1. Dave Winfield, baseball player for the New York Yankees, possibly the highest paid sportsman in the world, receives $94,000 (£49,000) for each of his team's regular-season games. In addition, escalating clauses bring in a further $1.5 million per year.

2. In 1981 the Internazionales Milan football club offered the Brazilian club, Flamengo, a transfer fee of £936,000 to sell the services of Zico, the most famous Brazilian player since Pelé – who was earning around $1 million a year from the New York Cosmos before his retirement. Zico was offered £624,000 to sign and £520,000 a year to play for three years, but he would not leave his home and fans at Rio de Janeiro's Maracana stadium – the world's largest stadium. So Coca-Cola Brazil and Flamengo came up with £780,000 a year for two years and Zico accepted that, along with his status as national hero.

At the last available date at the end of 1983:

3. The five top male tennis players in the world are:

John McEnroe	$941,000 (£489,320)
Ivan Lendl	$716,037 (£372,339)
Jimmy Connors	$395,872 (£205,853)
Guillermo Vilas	$387,261 (£201,376)
José Luis Clerc	$317,375 (£165,035)

4. The five top female tennis players in the world are:

Martina Navratilova	$865,437 (£450,027)
Chris Evert Lloyd	$572,162 (£297,524)
Tracy Austin	$453,409 (£235,772)
Andrea Jaeger	$392,115 (£203,900)
Pam Shriver	$366,350 (£190,502)

5. The five top earners in the sport of professional golf are:

Tom Kite	$375,699 (£195,363)
Raymond Floyd	$359,360 (£186,867)
Tom Watson	$347,660 (£180,783)
Bruce Lietzke	$343,446 (£178,592)
Bill Rogers	$314,411 (£164,013)

6. The sport of cycling can make a man big muscles and big pay cheques. The best place to earn is the Tour de France where it is said one third of the population of France will turn out to watch. The two superstars in this field are Eddie Merkx from Belgium and Bernard Hinault from France. Eddie Merkx has an estimated income from winnings and promotional work of 100 million Belgian francs or about £1.56 million. Hinault has won the Tour de France three times and his income runs to about 6 million francs – or £560,000 a year.

7. The highest-paid professional wrestler is Kanii Antonio Inoki of Japan who received $2,000,000 for his bout against Muhammad Ali in 1976.

Section Six

BANKS

Banks and banking operate under the exact same precept as all other business and commerce: 'Do other men, for they would do you.' The only difference in the banking business is that it is all done with the utmost respectability: 'Even honesty is a financial speculation.'

Till-tales untold

A bank is a bank is a bank.

Banks are generally regarded as either boring or frightening, depending on whether we give our money to them or borrow our money from them.

But banks have their stories too, and here is a selection of them which might serve to brighten their appeal or lessen their effect.

First, a few statistics:

1. Sixty-one per cent of all UK adults have a bank current account or chequing account and in the past five years there has been a 40 per cent increase in such accounts.

2. Seventy-three per cent of adults have an account of some kind with a bank and 50 per cent of adults have accounts with building societies.

3. Only 15 per cent of adults have no account of any kind anywhere. This last percentage amounts to 16.5 million people.

4. Eighty per cent of payments by bank current account holders are in cash.

Second, a few basic facts about banks:

1. There are three reasons (ostensibly) for the existence of banks:

– Providing a safe place to store valuables.

– As a source from which to borrow money.

– As the means of settling debts without having to carry large sums of cash around.

2. Several hundred years ago these needs were provided by the local goldsmiths, with whom people would leave their gold and valuables for safekeeping, in return for receipts. Eventually the goldsmiths realized that not all the gold and valuables would be withdrawn at once and that they could safely lend out portions of money for fixed periods at a profit. In addition it was possible for depositors to draw the value of their deposits in other countries to save transporting their assets long distances. Promissory notes were issued by the goldsmiths for value of deposits and these were given in payment of debts from person to person instead of the valuables themselves.

3. The cheque (or check in the US) arose about 300 years ago directly out of the use of exchanged receipts or promissory notes and were illegal to begin with and certainly regarded as highly immoral, but their convenience soon outweighed any moral considerations and the legalities soon followed.

4. Until 1931 there was a national responsibility not to issue more hard currency than could be backed up by gold deposits. So in effect, until that date if everyone handed in their notes for value, there would have been enough gold to go around.

Today, if we *all* tramped into our local 'listening banks' etc., and demanded our face-value gold, the banks and the nation would go bankrupt overnight. There is currently enough gold on deposit in the Bank of England's vaults to cover around one third of the issued currency. (It is no longer possible, in fact, to receive face-value gold.)

5. The biggest difference between a bank in the UK and a bank in the US is that in the UK, in order to open a bank account, it is necessary not only to have money but also to have friends. A reference provided by a bank-account holder must be furnished before a new account may be opened. The process, regardless of what the adverts tell us, takes about two weeks. In the US anyone can walk into almost any bank and open an account on the spot, receive a cheque book and use it, provided they deposit enough money in the account to cover the cheques. One of the reasons why this is so in New York State is that it is a crime to pay a cheque without having funds to back it. In the UK a bouncing cheque will not send you to prison.

In addition, in the US, with some of the competing banks, opening an account and depositing over a fixed amount of cash will bring you free gifts like cut glass or even a TV set. Roll on, competition amongst banks in the UK!

6. Banks all over the world lend money to each other. This is called the Interbank lending system and it occurs because the larger banks usually have more money on deposit than the smaller ones and all banks must balance their accounts each day – so they borrow and lend amongst themselves. So, if you leave a lot of money in your current account each day, even though the banks are not paying you any interest on that money they are making interest on it through the overnight Interbank lending market – about 11 per cent per annum in the UK. In the US almost all money in all accounts earns interest, if only at a low rate, and this system is slowly waking up in the UK, too, with various different names. No bank is doing anyone any favours with these accounts, they are simply reducing their profits slightly to attract more custom.

Now for the stories.

1. In 1980 there were 531,000 bank tellers in the US, and 220,000 in the UK. The teller's task is to count the cash and balance the till each day. In the UK, in an average year each of the large high-street-bank groups loses as much as £100 million through 'miss' accounting and bad debts. In 1983 the Midland Bank in the UK lost £2 million through the alleged excessive generosity of one manager! The poor man was arrested and charged with fraud and false accounting.

2. Big bank notes are now becoming a rarity with the rapid advent of electronic and plastic money. The largest notes printed were not today's. In the 1980s it is hard to find a $1000 bill and the largest UK note available in circulation is only £50. The last $10,000 bill was printed in 1944. In 1812 two bank notes were printed for one million pounds each, largely for internal accounting procedures. They would have been hard to cash but are still in existence. The highest issued denomination notes in the UK were £1000, printed for the first time in 1725 and discontinued in 1943. They were finally withdrawn in April 1945 but by all accounts there are still sixty-three of them unaccounted for.

3. Most of the large banks keep or have access to black lists. We all live in fear and trepidation of being placed on such lists – a bit like catching the plague. It is in fact harder than you might imagine to get on a black list, but here are two of the ways it can happen:
– If an individual fails to pay a debt after between two months and a year, the bank or credit card company will issue local or high court proceedings against that individual. If the writ is not fulfilled then

judgement is issued and the offender goes on the court 'black' list. This list is available to anyone with a professional interest in the individual and can have an adverse effect on employment prospects and certainly will prevent the person on the list from acquiring further loans. The name can be removed from the list once the debt has been repaid in full, for the payment of a small fee.

– The lesser-known black list, operated by Barclays Bank and the Royal Bank of Canada, is euphemistically entitled 'List of unacceptable names'. Apart from the above-named banks the list is also kept by the FBI and the Swiss banks. If you get your name on this list and you're in the money business in any way, then buddy you got problems.

The categories on the list include: informants, flakes, non-producers, dealers, big talkers, hot promoters, super flakes, daisy-chainers, scam artists, frauds. Did you ever hear of such a bunch of scoundrels – fresh out of a pirate boat on the high seas!

A flake is not a chocolate bar but a money dealer who lies. A big talker is just that. A daisy-chainer plays the round-the-table party game, changing the facts as they go by, and a scam artist is one better than a fraud and worse than a flake. For fuller definitions turn to Section Three: words and phrases not in the dictionaries.

4. In 1983, at a small bank in California, an intrigue was unearthed in which a female bank teller aged eighteen and a customer, male, aged twenty-eight, were sending each other messages written on the backs of one-dollar bills. The messages took the form of coded numbers and letters which made no sense to the bank manager when the situation was drawn to his attention. The offending bank notes had been exchanged daily for the past month and only came to the manager's notice at the end of this period. He immediately called the police, expecting a robbery to take place with the cooperation of the female teller in the bank.

When the customer came in again with one of the annotated dollar bills in his hand to pay into his account, which now had over $30 in it, FBI agents grabbed the poor fellow and frogmarched him to the back of the bank. There waiting was the terrified eighteen-year-old girl.

After three hours of interrogation, the arrival of various parents and witnesses, the true story convinced the FBI agents and the manager to drop all suspicions. They were lovers and the girl's parents had forbidden any contact between them because of the age difference, so messages were necessary and the simplest and most logical notepaper was the bank's. Two days later the bank was robbed of $50,000 and the girl teller didn't turn up for work the following day.

5.   The bank with the largest number of employees and the largest number of branches in the world is the State Bank of India. With assets of only $23 billion, low in the world ratings, it employs 228,000 people and has over 8000 branches world wide.

6.   The largest bank vault in the world is in the Chase Manhattan building in New York. Its six doors weigh forty tons each but may easily be closed with the tip of a finger. The vault measures 350 × 100 × 8 feet and weighs 879 tons.

7.   There are many very small banks throughout the world – most of them strictly speaking only licensed deposit takers. One of the very smallest is City Bank Trust which operates in London out of a semi-detached terraced house in the West End. It was originally owned under another name by John Stonehouse, the man who disappeared from a beach, thought drowned, but turned up in Australia, without his bank!

8. In the United States of America during 1982 and 1983, particularly in the West Coast area, there were literally thousands of bank robberies. At one period it became a fashion for people from various parts of the country to go to Los Angeles just to rob a bank. These were not 'robbers' with criminal records, or even experts in the field in any way. They were ordinary people who simply wanted to make a fast buck and return to their normal lives thereafter. It was so easy that family men would don a stocking, buy a fake gun and walk out of a bank $50,000 richer. The banks would simply claim against their insurance and it was cheaper to do this than spend hundreds of thousands of dollars on security and risk lives in trying to stop the robberies. During 1984 the fashion seems to have passed.

9. On 17 August 1984 there was a total in notes and coinage in circulation in the United Kingdom of £11,456,519,229. This sum varies from month to month according to what the Treasury needs to have available. In addition, on that date there was a further £3,480,771 in the banking sector in the form of retained currency. In the United States the total figure was 164,102,000,000 on approximately the same date.

world top banks

The list of the world's largest banks is published in various international journals and varies each year according to financial fluctuations. The following is the top 100 and is accurate to within a few million (!) as at 1984.

Bank	Assets	Employees
Citicorp, New York	$120,680,000,000	60,600
Bank American Corp., San Francisco	$115,242,000,000	85,266
Bank National de Paris	$109,944,000,000	51,299
Credit Agricole, Paris	$98,507,000,000	70,790
Credit Lyonnais, Paris	$96,735,000,000	45,471
Barclays Group, London	$95,328,000,000	120,000
National Westminster Bank, London	$87,967,000,000	88,000
Dai-Ichi Kangyo Bank, Tokyo	$86,925,000,000	23,684
Société Générale, Paris	$85,742,000,000	46,462
Fuji Bank, Tokyo	$83,744,000,000	18,584
Deutsche Bank, Frankfurt	$83,394,000,000	45,168
Mitsubishi Bank, Tokyo	$80,799,000,000	18,544
Sumitomo Bank, Osaka	$80,684,000,000	15,500
Midland Bank, London	$77,493,000,000	91,400

Chase Manhattan Corp., NY	$77,050,000,000	36,810
Sanwa Bank, Osaka	$74,778,000,000	17,192
Royal Bank of Canada, Montreal	$69,324,000,000	39,757
Bank of Tokyo	$64,646,000,000	14,502
Banco Brasil, Brasilia	$61,739,000,000	119,413
Manufacturers Hanover Corp., NY	$60,113,000,000	
Industrial Bank of Japan, Tokyo	$59,866,000,000	5370
Dresdner Bank, Frankfurt	$57,608,000,000	30,949
Mitsui Bank, Tokyo	$57,331,000,000	12,284
Hongkong & Shanghai Bank, HK	$57,132,000,000	18,853
Norinchukin Bank, Tokyo	$56,499,000,000	3064
Westdeutsche Landesbank, Dusseldorf	$55,770,000,000	7436
Lloyds Bank, London	$55,630,000,000	70,229
J. P. Morgan, NY	$54,695,000,000	12,711
Tokai Bank, Japan	$54,020,000,000	14,050
Canadian Imperial Bank of Commerce, Toronto	$53,400,000,000	34,955
Union Bank of Switzerland, Zurich	$53,323,000,000	16,988
Banque Paripas, Paris	$51,584,000,000	
Swiss Bank Corp, Basle	$48,541,000,000	14,332
Bank of Montreal	$48,109,000,000	29,866
Long-term Credit Bank of Japan	$47,224,000,000	3607
Algemene Bank Nederland, Amsterdam	$47,222,000,000	28,453
Chemical Bank, NY	$45,530,000,000	19,535

Mitsibishi Trust Corp., Tokyo	$45,301,000,000	6445
Commerzbank, Frankfurt	$45,108,000,000	21,393
Taiyo Kobe Bank, Tokyo	$44,873,000,000	14,807
Banca Nazionale del Lavoro, Rome	$44,418,000,000	22,190
Bayerische Vereinsbank, Munich	$44,369,000,000	12,641
Amsterdam-Rotterdam Bank, Amsterdam	$42,608,000,000	23,797
Continental Illinois Corp., Chicago	$42,209,000,000	12,930
Rabobank, Utrecht	$41,973,000,000	28,020
Bank of Nova Scotia, Halifax	$41,903,000,000	26,240
Sumitomo Trust & Banking, Osaka	$41,254,000,000	6345
Mitsubishi Trust Corp., Tokyo	$40,343,000,000	5829
Banca Commerciale Italiana, Milan	$39,992,000,000	22,860
Bayerische Landesbank, Munich	$39,710,000,000	4067
First Interstate Bancorp, LA	$39,330,000,000	31,903
Standard Chartered Bank, London	$39,241,000,000	55,493
Banco di Roma, Italy	$39,127,000,000	16,691
Bayerische Hypotheken und Wechsel Bank, Munich	$38,743,000,000	11,481
Daiwa Bank, Osaka	$38,133,000,000	11,097
Bankers Trust, New York	$37,805,000,000	11,906

Crédit Suisse, Zurich	$36,850,000,000	12,495
Security Pacific Corp., LA	$34,793,000,000	27,058
Toronto-Dominion Bank, Toronto	$34,761,000,000	18,333
First Chicago Corp., Chicago	$34,410,000,000	11,341
Caripio, Milan	$32,664,000,000	12,490
Société Générale de Banque, Brussels	$32,661,000,000	15,445
Istituto Bancario San Paolo di Torino, Turin	$30,990,000,000	13,680
Yasuda Trust & Banking, Tokyo	$29,733,000,000	5133
Nippon Credit Bank, Tokyo	$29,127,000,000	1828
Deutsche Genossen- schaftsbank, Frankfurt	$29,090,000,000	2215
Kyowa Bank, Tokyo	$28,849,000,000	10,588
Credito Italiano, Milan	$28,589,000,000	18,535
Monte dei Paschi di Siena, Siena	$28,563,000,000	15,043
Westpac Banking Corp., Sydney	$27,697,000,000	40,097
Banque Indosuez, Paris	$27,244,000,000	8622
Bank Melli Iran, Teheran	$27,057,000,000	17,523
Shoko Chukin Bank, Tokyo	$26,473,000,000	7318
Crédit Industriel et Commercial, Paris	$25,988,000,000	24,824
Saitama Bank, Urawa, Japan	$25,725,000,000	8960
Norddeutsche Landes- bank, Hanover	$24,417,000,000	4800

Hessische Landesbank, Frankfurt	$24,188,000,000	2879
Wells Fargo, San Francisco	$24,028,000,000	17,100
Bank für Gemein- wirtschaft, Frankfurt	$23,675,000,000	8097
State Bank of India, Bombay	$23,556,000,000	228,518
Toyo Trust & Banking, Tokyo	$23,208,000,000	4877
Nederlandsche Middestandsbank, Amsterdam	$22,690,000,000	10,948
Bank Leumi Le-Israel, Tel Aviv	$22,028,000,000	15,649
Commonwealth Banking Corp., Sydney	$21,450,000,000	32,357
Hokkaido Takushoku Bank, Sapporo	$21,437,000,000	7520
Banque Bruxelles Lambert, Brussels	$21,230,000,000	11,507
InterFirst Corp., Dallas	$21,030,000,000	8520
Banco Espanol de Credito, Madrid	$20,868,000,000	25,390
Banco Central, Madrid	$20,782,000,000	26,524
Bank Hapoalim, Tel Aviv	$20,594,000,000	10,263
Bank of Yokohama	$20,395,000,000	7638
Creditanstalt- Bankverein, Vienna	$19,573,000,000	9169
Skandinaviska Enskilda Banken, Stockholm	$19,133,000,000	7110

Kredietbank, Brussels	$19,121,000,000	10,335
Banco di Napoli, Naples	$18,992,000,000	13,168
Mellon National Corp., Pittsburgh	$18,818,000,000	
Groupe des Banques Populaires, Paris	$18,729,000,000	26,965
Crédit Communal de Belgique, Brussels	$18,669,000,000	2722
Rafidain Bank, Baghdad	$18,562,000,000	12,546
Irving Bank Corp., NY	$18,375,000,000	9600

interesting comparisons about the world's top banks

1. Out of the world's top banks there are five British banks, with total assets of $355,659 billion, twenty-two Japanese banks with total assets of $1,161,367 billion. The interesting thing about comparing the two countries' banking power is not the number of banks with such assets but the quantity of staff employed.

In the five British banks in the top 100 list there are 425,122 people employed. Within the Japanese banks, all twenty-two of them, there are but 226,222 employees – that's just under half as many employees producing three times as much money. Does this mean, we ask ourselves, that the diminutive Japanese bank employee is six times more energetic than the British?

2. Per capita power in the banking world goes as follows:

In the US a bank employee makes $1.95 million of assets per annum.

In Japan a bank employee makes $5.13 million of assets per annum.

In the UK a bank employee makes $0.83 million assets per annum.

In Germany a bank employee makes $2.89 million assets per annum.

In France a bank employee makes $1.41 million assets per annum.

3. The State Bank of India produced, during the year ending mid 1983, $23,556,000,000 using 228,518 employees, the largest number of employees in any bank in the world – $103,315 per bank employee.

4. There are approximately eight million people employed in the top five hundred banks throughout the world and around five billion people in the world – so, another piece of useless information – the world of major banking consumes around 0.16 per cent of world population.

Plastic money

Most of the modern credit cards are controlled by the banks or banking-related organizations. Lending money, as we have seen in 'Till-tales untold', is the business of the bank, that's how they make their profits. Credit cards make more profits than almost any other form of lending with interest rates of over 25 per cent per annum in many cases.

So, here is the plastic money list:

1. Some statistics and facts:

– In the UK during 1983 there were the following cards in issue:

Barclaycard	6,500,000
Access	5,600,000
Trustcard	1,800,000
American Express	700,000
Diners Club	300,000
Others	100,000

In addition there were 4,500,000 store cards, used for extended credit, subscription accounts etc., in British stores. That made a total of 19,500,000 credit cards in the UK – 35 per cent of the country's total population, though of course many people carry around one of each of the major cards so we cannot say that 35 per cent of the population has a credit card. Nevertheless if you think that at any one time there must be something like an average of £300 per person, per credit card owing to the credit card companies that makes a total of £6000 million in loans. Such loans are 'floating' in and out of credit all of the time and a surprisingly small number of people leave their credit cards unpaid for more than a month. Nevertheless, credit card profits for 1983 were astronomical.

– On 15 February 1983 the *Sunday Express* magazine published a comparison chart of the eight different credit cards in use in the UK today. Here is that chart reproduced:

	Amex (green)	Diners	Barclaycard	Access	Trustard	Amex (gold)	Barclays (prem)	Midland (gold)
UK launch	1964	1951	1966	1972	1978	1981	1982	1982
UK holders	700,000	260,000	6.5 m	6 m	1.8 m	50,000	N/A	27,000
UK Merchants	50,000	43,000	187,000	189,000	187,000	50,000	187,000	189,000
World Merch.	600,000	500,000	+3.5 m	4 m	3.5 m	600,000	3.5 m	4 m
World cash facilities	Amex travel offices	3,300	125,000 Visa banks	60,000 banks	125,000 banks	Amex & Lloyds	125,000 Visa banks	60,000 banks
Credit limit	None	None	Av. £500	Av. £600	Av. £400	None	None	None
Min. salary	£8000	£10,000	None	Varies	Varies	£20,000	£20,000	£20,000 suggested
Av. salary	£19,000	£20,000	None	None	£7,750	£35,000	No figure	No figure
Bank ac.	Any bank	Any bank	Any bank	Any bank	Any bank	Any bank	Any bank	Any bank
Fee	£17.50	£10	None	None	None	£40	£40	£40
Ann sub.	£17.50	£17.50	None	None	None	£40	£40	£40
Merch. fee	None	None	£20	£30	£20	None	None	None
Merch. disc.	2–5%	3.5–6%	2–4½%	4%	2–4½%	2–5%	2–4½%	1–4%

Payment due	Immediate	Immediate	25 days	25 days	25 days	Immediate	25 days	25 days
Min. payment	In full	In full	£5 or 5%	£5 or 5%	£5 or 5%	In full	In full	In full
Interest	None (2% over base after 60 days)	None (2% over base after 40 days)	None if paid in full	$1\frac{3}{4}\%$ on unpaid amount	$1\frac{3}{4}\%$ on unpaid amount	None (2% over base after 60 days)	None (except on unpaid amount after 25 days)	$2\frac{1}{4}\%$ on unpaid amount
Cash (home)	No	No	Any amount within limit	Any amount within limit	Any amount within limit	No	£7500	Any amount up to facility
Cash (abroad)	No	Local limits	£100 p. day	£100 p. day	£100 p. day	No	£250 p. day	£100 p. day
Cheque cash	£50–£100	£50	£50–£100	No	£100 p. day	£300–£750	£250 p. day	£250 p. day
Cheque cash (abroad)	£100–£400	$1000 p. 2 w.	£100 p. day	No	£100 p. day	£1000 p. w.	£250 p. day	£250 p. day
Service till	No	No.	£100 p.w.	£100 p.w.	No	£300 p. day	£100 p. day	£100 p.w.
Trave. cheques	Yes	Yes	Yes	Yes	Yes	Yes	Yes	Yes

	Amex (green)	Diners	Barclaycard	Access	Trustcard	Amex (gold)	Barclays (prem)	Midland (gold)
Cheque guar.	No	No	Yes	No	Yes	No	Yes	No
Auto travel insurance	£35,000	£50,000	£15,000	£15,000	£20,000	£150,000	£15,000	£150,000
Extra cards	Yes	Yes	Yes	Yes	Yes	Yes	Yes	Yes
Company cards	Yes	Yes	Yes	Yes	Yes	No	No	No

EXTRAS:

Amex (green): Bulletins. No-deposit car hire. Amex travel service. Hotel reservations assured. 'Be my guest' absent host service. 24-hour emergency phone service.

Diners: Magazine. Free accident cover. Free all-risk on purchases for 15 days. Free overseas policy with £1200 charged in previous 12 months. 15% BUPA discount. Guaranteed hotel reservations. Cigar, whisky and floral service.

Barclaycard: Magazine. Masterloan unsecured. Personal loan.

Trustcard: 10% discount and guarantee of car at Swan National. 25% discount on BUPA and PPP plans.

Amex (gold): Min. unsecured overdraft of £7500 at Lloyds at max. 2$^{1}/_{2}$% over base. Emergency advice. City Guides. Business information. Others as for Green card.

Barclays (premier): Min. unsecured overdraft at Barclays of £7500 – 2$^{1}/_{2}$% over base. Free use of strong room. Use of phone, telex etc., in major Barclays branches. Financial consultation. Help abroad.

Midland (gold): Min. unsecured overdraft £7500 at Midland, 9% discount at some hotels. Discount on car hire. Help abroad. Meet and Greet service at Heathrow and Gatwick.

plastic money stories

1. The latest idea for plastic money development is the do-everything go-anywhere pay-and-store credit card. The card will probably be in general use before the end of the century and will be exactly the size of the modern credit card, no thicker and no larger. It will carry a small liquid crystal screen on which the carrier can check his credit line, directly linked to his bank account, from which each payment is immediately and directly drawn whenever he purchases an item or draws cash from a machine. The card is linked by short-wave transmission to a computer which keeps the card's accounts and pays the credit company or the store for each use, thus saving a fortune in collection costs. The card is also a calculator, an identity system and a direction finder, and may be used in a limited way to obtain general information regarding travel and currencies, and local information. It will book a hotel for you, rent a car in advance, book and pay for flights etc., all at the touch of tiny symbols on its face.

The card would naturally be useless to anyone else as it will only function upon touch of the owner, through sub-microscopic sensor cells in the surface of the plastic. The whole mechanism would be like a fine plastic sandwich, with the centre portion made up of very low-density material, micro-chips which would contain the transmission, a mini computer/calculator and the liquid crystal screen. Neat, eh?

2. Going a step further into the future, the next stage of plastic money may be in the brain itself! Experiments have already been planned to inject an interfaced computer into the brain; it would literally grow into the brain cells and work in conjunction with the brain. It would contain a full computer link, short-wave transmission capabilities and calculator functions, and be linked with the credit companies and banks. All you will need to do then is think-spend – window shopping may become hazardous!

3. It is projected that by the year 1994 75 per cent or more of the world's Western population will own and use at least one credit card regularly for the majority of leisure spending. This would make the credit card organizations second in the line of 'richest in the world' moguls. Presently the oil-producing nations have the richest groups, but the author predicts that those who ultimately control the spending of the individual will follow the Arabs and eventually buy them out. The banker will one day be our high priest and control our governments. Money is already a religion, soon it will become a total power, so build your fallout shelters, quick!

4. According to reports dated November, 1983 the man with the largest number of credit cards in the world is the American, Walter Cavanagh, who was born in 1943 and owns 1122 different credit cards with a total credit value of one and a quarter million dollars. His wallet holding the cards weighs 35 pounds.

5. A certain Saudi prince visited the London boat show at Earls Court, and took a fancy to the largest and most luxurious yacht there. He approached the salesman who attended the magnificent yacht and asked the price. It was £380,000. The prince requested the attendent to reserve him the yacht and handed over his Gold American Express Card. The attendant laughed and said that he doubted it would be possible to pay for such a large sum by credit card. The prince was unperturbed and suggested the attendent should telephone the credit agency. This was done. When the attendent read out the number on the card to the agency, he got one answer to his query regarding the credit limit on the card: 'Unlimited.'

6. A Mr Joachim De Matteis from the United States was staying in a luxury hotel in Geneva, in the presidential suite which cost around 3000 swiss francs a night (about £1000). He had been there for nearly a month and when he produced his credit card (American Express) it was out of date and the hotel refused to call the agency, refused to let Mr De Matteis out of his room, refused the use of a telephone and in fact refused to cooperate or help the poor fellow at all. They called the police and planned to have him thrown in jail. However, Mr De Matteis managed to find a telephone which worked and made one call. Nine hours after his call, the president of American Express in New York arrived at the reception desk of the luxury hotel with Mr De Matteis' new credit card and presented it to the hotel manager along with his corporate credentials. The following month the hotel agreed to pay for the cost of this personal service!

18

dollar:sterling rates through history

In the 1980s we've become used to hearing that the dollar against the pound varies dramatically. But it wasn't at all like that before 1972. So, here is a list of random dates and the dollar:pound sterling comparisons, together with a reason or two for the changes.

1776	Following the War of Independence	£ = $ 4.50–5.00
1864	All-time peak during US Civil War	£ = $12.00
1880–1914	Fixed parity	£ = $ 4.86
Dec. 1916	Pegged rate, First World War	£ = $ 4.76
Feb. 1920	Low point after floating pound	£ = $ 3.40
Apr. 1925	Britain returns to gold standard	£ = $ 4.86
Nov. 1932	Britain forced off gold standard	£ = $ 3.14½
Mar. 1934	Floating currency period	£ = $ 5.20
Sept. 1939	Second World War fixed rate	£ = $ 4.03
Sept. 1949	Post Second World War devaluation	£ = $ 2.80

Nov. 1967	Second post Second World War devaluation	£ = $	2.40
Aug. 1971	Convertibility of USD to Gold	£ = $	2.42
June 1972	Pound re-floated	£ = $	2.58
Mar. 1976	Pound broke $2 barrier	£ = $	1.99
Oct. 1976	'All-time low' (or so they thought)	£ = $	1.56
Aug. 1978	Pound breaks back	£ = $	2.00
Dec. 1979	Iranian crisis	£ = $	2.19
Mar. 1985	All-time low	£ = $	1.03

The world's exchange rates

The world's currency rates, measured against the UK pound and the US dollar, change on a daily basis, for example, between early and late July 1984 the dollar changed against the UK pound from Dls 1.6 to 1.25. The following list is for general interest and particularly for those countries not normally published in banks. It may not therefore be exactly accurate but will give a good idea of the average figures.

Country	£	$
USA (dollar)	Anything between 1.03 and 1.06	
Canada (dollar)	2.18	1.24
Australia (dollar)	1.75	1.00

Japan (yen)	449.5	260.12
New Zealand (dollar)	2.37	1.34
Austria (schilling)	30.04	17.37
Belgium (franc)	81.5	47.16
Denmark (krone)	14.82	8.58
Finland (markka)	8.22	4.73
France (franc)	11.88	6.88
West Germany (mark)	4.27	2.47
Iceland (krona)	19.95	11.39
Italy (lire)	2392.00	1379.00
Luxembourg (franc)	81.5	47.16
Netherlands (guilder)	4.71	2.73
Norway (krona)	11.45	6.65
Spain (peseta)	194.6	112.3
Sweden (krona)	10.6	6.12
Switzerland (franc)	3.62	2.10
UK sterling (pound)		0.58
Algeria (dinar)	8.13	4.64
Indonesia (rupiah)	1158.00	661.5
Iran (rial)	146.5	84.0
Iraq (dinar)	0.51	0.29
Kuwait (dinar)	0.51	0.29
Libya (dinar)	0.51	0.29
Nigeria (naira)	1.17	0.67
Oman (rial)	0.60	0.35
Qatar (riyal)	6.37	3.64
Saudi Arabia (riyal)	6.02	3.44
United Arab Emirates (dirham)	6.42	3.67
Venezuela (bolivar)	7.52	4.29
Benin (franc)	594.12	344.25
Botswana (pula)	1.91	1.11
Burundi (franc)	156.3	90.00
Cameroon (franc)	594.12	344.25
Cape Verde (escudos)	95.85	54.70
Central African Rep. (franc)	594.12	344.25
Chad (franc)	594.12	344.25

Comoro Islands (franc)	594.12	344.25
Congo (franc)	594.12	344.25
Djibouti (franc)	300.00	177.72
Ethiopia (birr)	3.54	2.04
Gabon (franc)	594.12	344.25
Gambia (dalasi)	4.0	2.30
Ghana (cedi)	4.79	2.75
Guinea (syli)	39.5	22.71
Guinea–Bissau (peso)	70.45	40.47
Ivory Coast (franc)	594.12	344.25
Kenya (shilling)	18.95	10.98
Lesotho (maloti)	2.00	1.15
Liberia (dollar)	1.60	1.00
Madagascar (franc)	594.12	344.25
Malawi (kwacha)	1.93	1.10
Mali (franc)	1188.00	688.5
Mauritania (ouguiya)	89.90	51.29
Mauritius (rupee)	19.12	11.03
Morocco (dirham)	10.60	6.15
Niger (franc)	594.12	344.25
Rwanda (franc)	160.03	92.84
Sao Tome (dobra)	72.45	41.62
Senegal (franc)	594.12	344.25
Seychelles (rupee)	11.39	6.63
Sierra Leone (leone)	2.18	1.26
Somalia (shilling)	21.83	12.46
South Africa (rand)	2.00	1.15
Sudan (pound)	1.57	0.89
Swaziland (lilangeni)	2.50	1.51
Tanzania (shilling)	16.52	9.49
Togo (franc)	594.12	344.25
Tunisia (dinar)	1.05	0.60
Uganda (shilling)	170.0	98.75
Upper Volta (franc)	594.12	344.25
Zaire (zaire)	10.11	5.84
Zambia (kwacha)	1.63	0.94

Zimbabwe (dollar)	1.33	0.76
Argentina (peso)	38,014.00	20,500.00
Bahamas (dollar)	1.60	1.00
Barbados (dollar)	3.50	2.01
Bolivia (peso)	77.09	44.00
Brazil (cruzeiro)	319.28	182.25
Chile (peso)	80.58	46.17
Colombia (peso)	112.58	64.69
Costa Rica (colon)	66.57	38.13
Dominican Republic (peso)	1.60	1.00
Ecuador (sucre)	58.07	33.00
El Salvador (colon)	4.38	2.50
Guatemala (quetzal)	1.60	1.00
Guyana (dollar)	5.25	3.03
Haiti (gourde)	8.75	5.00
Honduras (lempira)	3.52	2.00
Jamaica (dollar)	3.12	1.78
Mexico (peso)	85.8	49.06
Neth. Antilles (guilder)	3.13	1.80
Nicaragua (cordoba)	17.51	10.05
Panama (balboa)	1.60	1.00
Paraguay (guarani)	220.72	126.00
Peru (sol)	1,171.00	701.32
Surinam (guilder)	3.14	1.78
Trinidad & Tobago (dollar)	4.20	2.40
Uruguay (new peso)	22.18	12.74
Afghanistan (afghani)	99.00	50.60
Bangladesh (taka)	38.25	22.00
Burma (kyat)	13.55	6.26
China (yuan)	3.35	1.92
Fiji (dollar)	1.65	0.94
India (rupee)	16.65	9.59
South Korea (won)	1,293.00	741.2
Malaysia (ringgit)	4.09	2.36
Nepal (rupee)	23.15	13.20
Pakistan (rupee)	21.09	12.16

Papua New Guinea (kina)	1.31	0.75
Philippines (peso)	14.64	8.50
Singapore (dollar)	3.73	2.14
Solomon Islands (dollar)	1.64	0.94
Sri Lanka (rupee)	36.36	20.90
Thailand (baht)	40.07	23.00
Cyprus (pound)	0.84	0.48
Greece (drachma)	120.13	69.60
Malta (pound)	1.39	0.79
Portugal (escudo)	147.5	85.15
Romania (leu)	7.95	4.47
Turkey (lira)	286.96	167.00
Yugoslavia (dinar)	85.16	48.67
Bahrain (dinar)	0.66	0.37
Egypt (pound)	1.55	0.88
Israel (shekel)	45.80	26.24
Jordan (dinar)	0.61	0.36
Lebanon (pound)	8.99	5.14
Syria (pound)	10.00	6.88
North Yemen (rial)	7.99	4.56
South Yemen (dinar)	0.60	0.35

Section Seven

VALUE OF THE WORLD

Some would say the world ain't worth the air it's polluted with and in a way they'd be right, for if you took an external Earth value it would be a little like the vacuum cleaner which sucks itself into oblivion. For us, of course, the value is intrinsic. There would be little point in an Earthman buying his own planet: where would he put the purchase price – into the banks he owned? But for an outsider, the planet's value might lie in its minerals or power sources or its people. But if they were going to pay us for our worth, it would have to be with materials which we need or do not have at all, in which case our value would alter. If a more advanced being came to Earth to trade, peacefully, probably the most valuable trading material he could bring with him would be knowledge. Advanced beings trade with primitive beings, knowledge for muscle.

15

things and their value

1. A piece of string – between ¹/₂p (1 cent) and £500,000,000 depending upon length.

2. An English 'White Fiver' – about £25.00 in London or $50 in US.

3. A glass of pure orange juice in Poona – 1 rupee plus three weeks of dysentery.

4. A gold Dupont lighter – £275 or $400.

5. A packet of untipped Camel cigarettes – £1.25 or $2.50.

6. A copy of the book *The Romance of Commerce* by H. Gordon Selfridge – £6.00.

7. An Exocet air-to-surface missile – £500,000.

8. A Hawkeye E-2C early warning aircraft – $34 million.

9. A pedigree German shepherd dog in London – £100.

10. A gold Sardinian 20-lire piece dated 1849 – £50.

11. A magnum of Grande Armée Fine Champagne Cognac, 1811 – £780.

12. A Sharp Elsi Mate EL-640 Voice synthesized clock and calculator – £50.

13. The cost of NASA's shuttle craft *Colombia*'s first trip from Earth – $9.9 billion.

14. One millionth of a microgramme of interferon – $10.

15. One bottle of 1822 Château Lafite – $31,000.

175

countries' Gross National Product

Now this is a tricky one. But in my introduction I promised to try to satisfy the alien visitor with some sort of world value. What would a creature from Alpha Centauri have to bring with him in the way of a bank balance if he wished to write a cheque for the planet Earth? Well, first of all he would probably have to settle the banks – a total value of all the cash and assets sitting in the banks of the world would cut his bank balance down a few shekels for starters, but then he would have to get to grips with the world's Gross National Product. So here, to begin with is a list of the world's production, set out country by country. The figures may vary slightly each year, up or down, but as at end of 1984 they are within a few million dollars.

Country	GNP	Population
Algeria	$36,600,000,000	19,100,000
Argentina	$55,000,000,000	27,900,000
Australia	$159,500,000,000	14,900,000

Brazil	$234,200,000,000	124,500,000
Canada	$279,200,000,000	24,300,000
China (1980)	$283,000,000,000	982,600,000
Cuba	$18,400,000,000	9,700,000
Egypt	$25,200,000,000	43,200,000
Ethiopia	$4,200,000,000	32,200,000
France	$568,300,000,000	54,100,000
East Germany (1980)	$120,900,000,000	16,700,000
West Germany	$678,700,000,000	61,700,000
India	$159,300,000,000	686,200,000
Indonesia	$66,800,000,000	150,880,000
Iran (1977)	$79,400,000,000	38,000,000
Israel	$20,600,000,000	4,000,000
Italy	$345,100,000,000	57,200,000
Japan	$1,127,000,000,000	118,500,000
Mexico	$170,000,000,000	71,900,000
Nigeria	$88,800,000,000	79,600,000
Pakistan	$28,000,000,000	82,500,000
Philippines	$38,900,000,000	49,500,000
Poland (1980)	$139,800,000,000	35,900,000
South Africa	$75,900,000,000	30,100,000
South Korea	$65,700,000,000	38,700,000
Spain	$186,200,000,000	37,700,000
Thailand	$36,000,000,000	48,100,000
Turkey	$57,300,000,000	45,700,000
United Kingdom	$480,400,000,000	56,000,000
USA	$2,925,500,000,000	230,800,000
USSR (1980)	$1,212,000,000,000	267,600,000
Vietnam (1978)	$8,900,000,000	54,900,000
Yugoslavia	$16,500,000,000	22,500,000
Zaire	$4,900,000,000	28,300,000

So, the total Gross National Product of the thirty-four major countries in the world comes to $9,796,200,000,000.

Then we come to the second-tier countries:

Country	GNP	Population
NORTH AFRICA		
Libya	$25,700,000,000	3,100,000
Malta	$1,200,000,000	360,000
Morocco	$14,900,000,000	20,700,000
Tunisia	$8,100,000,000	6,500,000
SAHEL		
Burkina Faso (Upper Volta)	$947,000,000	7,100,000
Mali	$1,106,000,000	7,200,000
Mauritania	$752,100,000	1,700,000
Niger	$1,744,000,000	5,500,000
Chad	$488,000,000	4,600,000
FAR WEST AFRICA		
Cape Verde	$100,000,000	329,000
Gambia	$150,000,000	619,000
Guinea	$1,590,000,000	5,600,000
Guinea-Bissau	$130,000,000	807,000
Liberia	$980,000,000	2,040,000
Senegal	$2,309,000,000	5,807,000
Sierra Leone	$950,000,000	3,570,000
GULF OF GUINEA		
Benin	$1,080,000,000	3,600,000
Ivory Coast	$8,510,000,000	8,300,000
Ghana	$4,920,000,000	12,100,000
Togo	$1,020,000,000	2,700,000
CENTRAL AFRICA		
Cameroon	$5,660,000,000	8,648,000
Central African Republic	$680,000,000	2,344,000
Congo	$325,000,000	1,600,000
Gabon	$2,420,000,000	660,000
Equatorial Guinea	$50,000,000	370,000
Sao Tome	$60,000,000	120,000

EAST AFRICA

Burundi	$830,000,000	4,190,000
Kenya	$6,650,000,000	17,220,000
Uganda	$3,750,000,000	13,600,000
Rwanda	$1,290,000,000	5,100,000
Tanzania	$6,130,000,000	18,500,000

NORTH EAST AFRICA

Djibouti	$170,000,000	381,000
Somalia	$470,000,000	3,763,000

NILE VALLEY

Sudan	$8,600,000,000	18,900,000

SOUTH TROPICAL AFRICA

Angola	$3,320,000,000	10,700,000
Malawi	$1,530,000,000	6,100,000
Mozambique	$2,810,000,000	10,700,000
Zambia	$3,840,000,000	6,000,000
Zimbabwe	$5,440,000,000	7,600,000

SOUTHERN AFRICA

Botswana	$800,000,000	850,000
Lesotho	$520,000,000	1,370,000
Namibia	$1,420,000,000	1,040,000
Swaziland	$380,000,000	570,000

INDIAN OCEAN

Comores	$100,000,000	370,000
Madagascar	$3,030,000,000	8,960,000
Maldives	$40,000,000	160,000
Mauritius	$1,020,000,000	940,000
Reunion	$2,010,000,000	530,000
Seychelles	$120,000,000	70,000

THE EAST

Iraq	$39,500,000,000	13,520,000
Jordan	$2,910,000,000	3,360,000
Lebanon	$1,280,000,000	2,630,000
Syria	$12,900,000,000	9,300,000
Saudi Arabia	$125,100,000,000	8,700,000

Oman	$5,280,000,000	920,000
North Yemen	$2,680,000,000	5,920,000
South Yemen	$810,000,000	1,950,000
Bahrain	$2,350,000,000	450,000
U.A.E.	$28,610,000,000	893,000
Kuwait	$24,270,000,000	1,353,000
Qatar	$6,020,000,000	231,000
Afghanistan	$3,500,000,000	16,360,000
SOUTH ASIA		
Bangladesh	$10,890,000,000	89,670,000
Bhutan	$105,000,000	1,320,000
Nepal	$1,900,000,000	15,000,000
Sri Lanka	$4,140,000,000	14,990,000
INDOCHINA		
Burma	$5,610,000,000	34,040,000
Kampuchea	$1,270,000,000	N.A.
Laos	$360,000,000	3,470,000
Thailand	$36,000,000,000	48,100,000
Vietnam (1978)	$8,900,000,000	54,900,000
SOUTH EAST ASIA		
Brunei	$2,620,000,000	230,000
Hong Kong	$21,500,000,000	5,240,000
Malaysia	$25,340,000,000	14,420,000
Singapore	$11,370,000,000	2,440,000
Taiwan	$32,300,000,000	18,200,000
NORTH EAST ASIA		
North Korea	$17,500,000,000	18,400,000
South Korea	$67,500,000,000	38,700,000
OCEANIA AND PACIFIC ISLANDS		
New Zealand	$24,000,000,000	3,100,000
Fiji	$1,160,000,000	640,000
Kiribati	$50,000,000	60,000
Nauru	N.A.	10,000
Papua New Guinea	$2,580,000,000	3,080,000
Samoa	$80,000,000	160,000

Solomon Islands	$110,000,000	240,000
Tonga	$50,000,000	100,000
Vanuatu	$60,000,000	120,000
CENTRAL AMERICA		
Belize	$160,000,000	150,000
Costa Rica	$3,820,000,000	2,260,000
El Salvador	$3,390,000,000	4,670,000
Guatemala	$8,640,000,000	7,210,000
Honduras	$2,710,000,000	3,820,000
Nicaragua	$2,230,000,000	2,760,000
Panama	$3,830,000,000	1,880,000
WESTERN CARIBBEAN		
Bahamas	$800,000,000	248,000
Dominican Republic	$6,900,000,000	5,584,000
Haiti	$1,500,000,000	5,102,000
Jamaica	$2,250,000,000	2,220,000
Puerto Rico	$11,070,000,000	3,785,000
EASTERN CARIBBEAN		
Barbados	$810,000,000	250,000
Dominica	$50,000,000	84,000
Grenada	$80,000,000	112,000
Guadeloupe	$1,270,000,000	329,000
Martinique	$1,510,000,000	324,000
St Lucia	$110,000,000	127,000
St Vincent	$60,000,000	109,000
Trinidad & Tobago	$5,110,000,000	1,182,000
VENEZUELA/GUYANAS		
Guyana	$540,000,000	802,000
French Guiana	$180,000,000	63,000
Surinam	$1,000,000,000	350,000
Venezuela	60,000,000,000	15,438,000
THE ANDES		
Bolivia	$5,940,000,000	5,710,000
Colombia	$36,800,000,000	27,280,000

Ecuador	$13,430,000,000	8,630,000
Peru	$19,890,000,000	18,100,000

THE SOUTH CONE

Chile	$27,400,000,000	11,300,000
Paraguay	$5,500,000,000	3,200,000
Uruguay	$9,200,000,000	3,000,000

EUROPE

Austria	$66,100,000,000	7,560,000
Liechtenstein	N.A.	26,000
Belgium	$97,500,000,000	9,870,000
Luxembourg	$3,700,000,000	365,000
Netherlands	$138,400,000,000	14,246,000
Denmark	$56,600,000,000	5,125,000
Greenland	$310,000,000	50,000
Finland	$48,300,000,000	4,789,000
Iceland	$2,800,000,000	227,000
Norway	$55,400,000,000	4,100,000
Sweden	$109,300,000,000	8,324,000
Ireland	$16,500,000,000	3,434,000
Andorra	N.A.	30,000
Monaco	N.A.	26,000
Portugal	$23,300,000,000	10,000,000
San Marino	N.A.	21,000
Cyprus	$2,100,000,000	600,000
Greece	$38,200,000,000	9,750,000
Albania	$2,200,000,000	2,795,000
Bulgaria	$37,390,000,000	8,892,000
Romania	$52,010,000,000	22,370,000
Hungary	$25,000,000,000	10,700,000
Czechoslovakia	$89,300,000,000	15,400,000

The total value of the rest of the world's Gross National Product comes to a grand $1,771,306,100,000 which is less than one-fifth of the GNP of the top thirty-four countries, and there are 141 countries in the second-tier list.

So the grand total for the section of the world which our visiting alien would have to cough up, to pay the full price of the world's ability to produce goods (presuming that the alien didn't wish to blast us all with his super ray gun) would be: $11,567,506,100,000. He might have some problems exchanging his Intergalactic credits for that many dollars, but if the world was desperate enough no doubt the Federal Reserve could arrange something.

The total population needed to produce this much product, according to the records is: 4,603,914,000 people.

Now, to divide one figure into the other, that means that for each person $2512.54 of national product was produced.

Section Eight

MONEY BUSINESS

All business is money business. There would
not be any point to having a business if it was
not to make money. The question is – how?
'The usual trade and commerce is cheating
all around by consent' (Thomas Fuller).

world's largest corporations

The following is a list of the top 100 industrial corporations, showing figures for turnover up to 1983.
Drawn from *The World View*.

Corporation	Turnover in $	Country
Exxon	108,108,000,000	US
Royal Dutch Shell	77,834,000,000	Anglo-Dutch
Mobil	64,448,000,000	US
General Motors	62,699,000,000	US
Texaco	57,628,000,000	US
British Petroleum	49,192,000,000	UK
Standard Oil California	44,224,000,000	US
Ford Motor	38,247,000,000	US
Standard Oil Indiana	29,947,000,000	US
IBM	29,070,000,000	US
Kuwait Petroleum	28,720,000,000	Kuwait
Gulf Oil	28,252,000,000	US
Atlantic Richfield	27,797,000,000	US
ENI	27,724,000,000	Italy

General Electric	27,240,000,000	US
Du Pont Industries	22,810,000,000	US
Unilever	22,707,000,000	Anglo-Dutch
VEBA	22,045,000,000	West Germany
Shell Oil	21,629,000,000	US
Total Oil	21,632,000,000	France
Petroleas de Venezuala	19,620,000,000	Venezuela
Fiat	18,463,000,000	Italy
Elf Aquitaine	18,347,000,000	France
BAT Industries	17,761,000,000	UK
Pemex	17,564,000,000	Mexico
Petrobras	17,452,000,000	Brazil
ITT	17,306,000,000	US
Philips	17,274,000,000	Netherlands
Volkswagen	16,894,000,000	West Germany
Daimler Benz	16,351,000,000	West Germany
Philips Petroleum	15,966,000,000	US
Nestlé	15,537,000,000	Switzerland
Tenneco	15,462,000,000	US
Renault	15,409,000,000	France
Hoechst	15,358,000,000	West Germany
Bayer	15,049,000,000	West Germany
Sun	15,012,000,000	US
Siemens	14,879,000,000	West Germany
Occidental Petroleum	14,708,000,000	US
Nippon Oil	14,589,000,000	Japan
Toyota Motor	14,225,000,000	Japan
BASF	14,167,000,000	West Germany
US Steel	13,941,000,000	US
United Technologies	13,668,000,000	US

Tokyo Electric	13,545,000,000	US
Standard Oil Ohio	13,457,000,000	US
Western Electric	13,008,000,000	US
Nissan Motor	12,997,000,000	Japan
Getty Oil	12,887,000,000	US
Peugeot	12,719,000,000	France
ICI	12,616,000,000	UK
Nippon Steel	12,585,000,000	Japan
Thyssen	12,126,000,000	West Germany
Dow Chemical	11,873,000,000	US
Proctor & Gamble	11,416,000,000	US
Chrysler	10,821,000,000	US
CAMPSA	10,780,000,000	Spain
Union Oil California	10,746,000,000	US
Canadian Pacific	10,652,000,000	Canada
Gasunie	10,563,000,000	Netherlands
Eastman Kodak	10,337,000,000	US
Petrofina	10,211,000,000	Belgium
Dart & Kraft	10,211,000,000	US
Union Carbide	10,168,000,000	US
Boeing	9,788,000,000	US
R. J. Reynolds	9,766,000,000	US
British Gas	9,609,000,000	UK
Matsuhita Electric	9,518,000,000	Japan
Amerada Hess	9,396,000,000	US
Westinghouse	9,368,000,000	US
National Coal Board	9,365,000,000	UK
Ashland Oil	9,262,000,000	US

Cities Serive	8,899,000,000	US
LTV	8,823,000,000	US
Beatrice Foods	8,773,000,000	US
Xerox	8,691,000,000	US
Hitachi	8,685,000,000	Japan
Volvo	8,629,000,000	Sweden
Rheinish-West. Elek	8,549,000,000	West Germany
Imperial Group	8,436,000,000	UK
Philip Morris	8,307,000,000	US
Stinnes	8,135,000,000	West Germany
Ruhr Kohle	8,126,000,000	West Germany
RCA	8,005,000,000	US
General Electric	7,745,000,000	UK
Thomson Brandt	7,671,000,000	France
Saint-Gobain- Pont-a-Mousson	7,642,000,000	France
Ciba-Geigy	7,618,000,000	Switzerland
Kansai Electric Power	7,533,000,000	Japan
Montedison	7,481,000,000	Italy
Naamloze Venootschap	7,464,000,000	Netherlands
Maruzen Oil	7,421,000,000	Japan
McDonnell Douglas	7,385,000,000	US
International Harvester	7,327,000,000	US
Bethlehem Steel	7,298,000,000	US
Pechiney Ugine Kuhlman	7,201,000,000	France
Hyundai Construction	7,131,000,000	South Korea

Rockwell		
International	7,040,000,000	US
Pepsico	7,027,000,000	US
Monsanto	6,948,000,000	US

biggest UK corporations

Turnovers in 1984:

1.	British Petroleum	£25,347,000,000
2.	Shell Transport and Trading	£15,846,000,000
3.	BAT Industries	£ 7,497,000,000
4.	Imperial Chemical Industry	£ 5,715,000,000
5.	Unilever	£ 4,345,800,000
6.	Imperial Group	£ 3,929,081,000
7.	Shell UK	£ 3,263,100,000
8.	Esso Petroleum	£ 3,219,400,000
9.	General Electric	£ 3,005,800,000
10.	Ford Motor	£ 2,924,000,000

things no one wants to know about tax

The way the world works is that we, the public, appoint our rulers and administrators to make the laws and see us through each year with, hopefully, the minimum of fuss and trouble. After we've appointed them, we pay money so that they can perform these duties efficiently and so that we can live without danger, drive comfortably on our roads, help those who are sick or needy, educate the young, and keep creature comforts working in our favour. In fact, we all know this does not always happen quite as well as it should, but then we don't always pay the taxes we should, so supposedly we have only ourselves to blame, which presumably could be applied to everything. But, when all is said and done, taxes are paid to keep the world running smoothly, though to look at how they actually work is as bizarre a section of any list of money items you can possibly imagine.

Here is a list of things, good, bad and indifferent, about taxes.

1. During 1980 the US Internal Revenue Service (IRS) received a total of 93,143,629 personal income tax returns. Of these 7 per cent or $6^1/_2$ million were wrongly filled out, 45 per cent showing too much tax and 55 per cent too little. The total amount of overpaid tax was $590,832,000 and the total underpaid was $1,119,633,000 – over twice as much.

The total tax collected during that year was $242,718,790,000 – that's *personal* income tax and does not, of course, include corporate taxes or local taxes.

There are 226,504,825 people in the US (or there were during 1980). This figure of course includes many who do not pay tax at all. If every single person in the US during that year had earned enough just to pay $1073 to the IRS, the same revenue would have been produced. As it was 93,143,629 paid an average of $2606 apiece.

2. The IRS spends $4.40 to collect every $1000 of taxes.

3. The full total revenues collected by the IRS during 1980 amounted to $465,871,222,000 – including taxes from individuals (52.1 per cent), corporate taxes (13.9 per cent), social security payments and excise, estate and unemployment insurance payments. That's an average of $2057 per inhabitant of the US.

4. At the bottom of every US tax return form a figure is given by the individual making the tax return which is in effect his or her income for that year. It is known as the adjusted gross income; i.e. the income after allowed deductions and expenses. The total gross adjusted income of all 93.14 million individuals who made returns was $1,606,265,685,000. This meant an average gross income over the whole of $17,158 apiece.

5. Out of the 93.14 million people returning, 73.7 million had actually to pay taxes – making the $242 billion mentioned above – an average therefore of $2600 (give or take!) per return taxed. Among those who paid no taxes there were actually six individuals who declared income between $500,000 and $1 million for the year and ten who declared incomes of over a million dollars for that year! Smart, huh?

6. There were 4112 people in the US who declared incomes of $1 million or more. Their total gross income for the period was $8,368,749,000 or $2,035,200 each, averaged out. Think about it – this means that in the US 0.001 per cent of the population gets 0.5 per cent of the total amount earned.

7. In Bahrain, Kuwait, Qatar and the island of Sark the level of taxation, regardless of income, is nil.

8. The country with the highest-ever rate of tax was Norway where over 2000 people paid more than 100 per cent of their taxable income in taxes. One shipping magnate, Hilmer Reksten, was assessed at nearly 500 per cent tax!

9. According to the *Guinness Book of Records* the highest recorded tax assessment of all time was $336 million levied on Howard Hughes' estate after his death.

10. Income tax came to the UK for the first time in 1799, to be levied on all incomes over £60 per annum! In 1842 the rate charged was 7d (2.91p) in the pound. It went down to 2d (0.83p) in the pound in 1875, its lowest level, and then climbed to 1s 3d (6.24p) in 1913. From April 1941 to 1946 the highest rate was reached for that period at 10s (50p) in the pound to aid the Second World War effort. The top rate now, of course, is 60 per cent, or 60p in the pound, and there ain't no war!

11. In the history of taxes, one of the most bizarre forms of tax levied was the window tax, much resented by the landed gentry, who promptly bricked up as large a proportion of their windows as was practical. There are still many London and major-city town houses with bricked windows, some of which have false windows painted on the outside to retain the semblance of the original architectural style.

12. Al Capone received eleven years' jail sentence for tax evasion and $80,000 in fines. He served eight years.

13. Sophia Loren was sentenced to thirty days in jail for failing to declare a tiny proportion of her 1970 income. After several years of exile she returned to Italy and the jail sentence, of which she was made to serve only seventeen days.

Section Nine

TIME IS MONEY

The only thing that really changes with regard to the passing of time and money is honour. As we grow more complex in business matters so the concept of honour diminishes. Why be honourable when you can make more money by dishonour? Nobody, after all, nowadays is going to challenge you to a duel so there is less risk of termination through dishonourable dealing – or is there? What about cancer, leukaemia and heart disease, to say nothing of constant stress? These are the natural results of dishonour, and as the world progresses into greater dishonour, into the next 'dark age', money will remain forever the same.

items of money in history

Money has been around for a long time. The first known currencies were issued in China around the seventh century BC and ever since then the only thing that has changed about it is its value. Here is a list of random money matters since the beginning of its time.

1. The use of gold as a monetary form predates written history, and its choice as a monetary system arises out of the fact that carting around cows and horses, pigs and animal pelts in order to acquire wheat and grain or fruit and vegetables is awkward, to say the least. In addition, it was felt almost impossible to find suitable barter levels that were consistent enough for any kind of convenience. You might go to town to buy a horse and take with you two cows. The fellow with the horse might demand three cows, or two cows and a goat, so you'd have to tramp all the way back to the farm and start all over again – by which time he would have sold the horse anyway. So people looked for a convenient intermediate substance to exchange horse for cow or whatever else. The reason for the choice of gold was its ease of transport (you can carry quite a lot of it without difficulty) its tendency to hold its value (there isn't that much of it, so its price does not fluctuate), its durability (it doesn't wear out), the fact that it is homogeneous (one unit is virtually identical with another), it can be manufactured into large or small coins. So, gold became the first and most popular commodity money.

2. The Great Fire of London, supposedly started at midday on 2 September 1666, destroyed nearly 80 per cent of all buildings within the City of London. Broken down to exact figures this worked out at 13,200 houses, 87 churches and over 400 streets. Contemporary housing prices rated the average terraced dwelling at around £75 in value, estimating on the basis of what would now be termed a freehold. To rebuild the churches would have cost around £5000 each and to re-lay and make good a street perhaps £40. This brings the cost of the Great Fire of London to around £1,441,000 – roughly what it costs to build about half of a modern office block today.

3. By contrast, on 18 April 1906, in the early hours before dawn in San Francisco, an earthquake lasting less than a minute destroyed 500 blocks, 28,000 buildings and 450 people. The total damage was estimated at $500 million. If it should ever happen again, striking exactly the same area and causing the same amount of damage, the cost would be in the order of $5 billion.

4. Public executions throughout history have been tremendous crowd pullers. Nowadays, of course, we are forced to transfer our passion for watching other people die on to television, video and perhaps local road accidents. The fees charged by execution organizers varied greatly according to how notorious the condemned was. Your average local thief would not attract more than a few pennies, if anything, but at the other end of the scale, assassins such as Charles

Guiteau, who was responsible for the death of President Garfield in 1882, attracted onlookers prepared to pay as much as $300 just to see him strangled.

5. Advertising costs within the television media are now well known; a few seconds costs a zillion dollars! By contrast, back in the dim and distant history of the box – to be precise, 1941 – a single twenty-second advertisement run by Bulova Watches cost exactly $9.

6. The very first American insurance policy for accidents was issued in 1864 by the Travelers Insurance Company to a Mr James Bolter. The policy was issued for $1000 and covered the journey which Mr Bolter took from the local post office to his home. The premium that he paid was 2 cents.

7. In about 1536 a Spaniard named Gonzalo Jiminez de Quesada explored Colombia and found a people who enjoyed a tradition of great value. The leader of the Chibchas people, before taking the throne, covered his body in resin and gold dust and took a bath in the local lake, watching the gold dust sink to the bottom. When the lake was drained in 1912 millions of dollars' worth of gold and treasure were found at the bottom.

8. In 1762 a man named John Harrison invented the marine clock (chronometer) which formed the basis of reliable measurement of longitude at sea until quite recent years. He received the sum of £20,000 from the British government for his work – a modern value would be about £2 million.

9. Some of the very earliest poetry of John Keats was published in the early nineteenth century in a local periodical, for which Keats earned 2 pence.

10. In the old West, during the times of Wyatt Earp, Buffalo Bill and Wild Bill Hickock, the bounty hunter, was one of the best-paid, least-loved characters roaming the arid landscapes. Unlike the *Star Wars* monsters, clad in three tons of armour and a Third World War armoury, the Western bounty hunter needed only a single six-shot hand gun which might have set him back between $20 and $50; a holster, maybe another $10 maximum; and a horse, probably around $40. So far around $100 a man could go out and catch himself a robber or two and earn between $500 and $5000 a head. An unsung anti-hero named Jeremiah Sangdon was reported to bring in an average of $7500 a year from bounty hunting, though for his troubles he ended up at the age of fifty-six, retired, with one ear missing, his heel blown off and only seven out of his original *eleven* fingers still in place. He was known for his fast draw and had a hand gun fitted especially with two triggers and a rapid chamber movement so that he could get two shots off faster than if he had two guns. Helped perhaps by the eleventh finger!

11. In 1968 the greatest annual budget expenditure of any country was that of the United States government. In 1983, the greatest annual budget expenditure was still made by the United States government. The only difference lies in the figures:

1968 $158,414 millions
1983 $768,800 millions

12. Overall world figures fairly closely reflect the same pattern: for expenditure from 1966/7 up to 1983 the increase is around 500 per cent. For worldwide Gross National Product, i.e. that which we produce to balance out our expenditure, the increase over the same period is around 410 per cent. Finally, the figures on private wealth, i.e. the value of all physical assets averaged out to a per capita amount, increased during the same period by only 230 per cent. More people, less money!

13. In 1250 gold was valued at 19 shillings per ounce; that's 90 pence or about $1. Its value today runs at about £380 or $500 per ounce.

14. The actual hard cash in circulation also increases in all countries. In the UK during 1967, to be precise on 22 December, there was £3,207,000,000 in circulation, printed and released by the Bank of England. On 22 December 1983 the figure was £11,865,799,605. Up until 1931 the money in circulation was supposed not to exceed the amount of gold on reserve. In 1967 the amount of gold on reserve in the Bank of England books was worth £1,118,000,000 – covering 34.86 per cent of the amount of money in use. In 1983 the gold reserves amounted to £4,583,000,000 – covering 38.62 per cent of the money in circulation.

Section Ten

SEX AND MONEY

The poor make love more than the rich. Give a woman too much money and she won't want to make love; starve her, and she'll have nothing better to do! There's a sexist remark if there ever was one, but of course the same applies to men. When the lights went out in New York City more people copulated because there was no TV, video, movies, fast food, etc., etc. Money stops the world going round. So, logically, as the world becomes wealthier and wealthier and contraception more and more efficient, we'll end up with a few million millionaires living alone, surrounded by technology.

The cost of a trick

Sex and money are closely allied and the commercial world operates with both as integral parts of its system. So here is a list of the cost of sex in its various available forms throughout the world.

1. Prostitution etc.

The cost of a 'trick'

In London:	Finchley	£25 for half an hour
	Mayfair	£35–50 for half an hour
	King's Cross	£10 for half an hour
	Soho	£25 for one hour
In New York:	42nd St	$30–50 for half an hour
	Harlem	$20 for one hour
	65th St	$100+ for one hour
		$500 for one night
Visits to hotels in Manhattan		$50–200 for one hour
In Bombay		$5 for one hour
In Hong Kong		$3–20 for one session
In Paris (Montmartre)		$50+ for one session
In Frankfurt		$100+ for one session – union protected rates!
In Rome		$25–50 for one session
In Chicago (high-class)		$50 for one hour

| In Amsterdam | $75 for one session |
| In Zurich (if you can find it) | $100 for one session |

Massage plus

It is hard to distinguish between genuine massage and relief massage in some cities. If the advertisement in a magazine or on the door of a suitably decorated establishment is obvious enough then you know what you're in for but some prostitution rackets are deliberately discrete and therefore less obvious.

2. London: Finchley   £25 for relief massage including hand and oral relief

        Mayfair   £25 for the same

        King's Cross   £5 for hand relief and £7–8 for oral relief, in the back seat of the car

        Soho   £10–£20.

2. Some men's magazines advertise visiting massage, which includes relief massage, for £20 plus, depending on the peculiarities of the requirements. For sexual intercourse the price (when available) would increase by anything from double to five times – depending on what the girl thinks the client is worth and how long she stays.

3. Massage parlours work out about the same as above except of course there is no travel cost!

Rates in other big cities tend to be similar in the Western Hemisphere and in the East a lot cheaper, except for Japan where the whole business is run like a German transport café or Swissair.

Sex shows

The categories of sex show are: peep, strip, live sex, nude encounter and photo-sessions, with possible variations on the basic themes.

Peep shows:

London (Soho)	50p for three minutes
New York (Manhattan)	$1 for two minutes
Amsterdam	$2 for two minutes
Munich	Dm5 for three minutes
Zurich	Sf5 for three minutes
Athens	$1 for three minutes
Tokyo	$2.50 for three minutes

The girls, usually in rotation or two at a time, parade on a stage behind small cubicles in which there are automatic slots which open upon payment of money into a coin slot. The girls are naked and show just about everything the female human body has to show.

In some of the peep-show parlours the girls will invite the men into separate compartments or rooms for other activities such as the nude encounter.

The nude encounter

Usually a small double cubicle with a glass or plastic division with holes in it so that both sides can hear one another and so that money can be passed through the division. The girl is naked inside her part and the man may either remain dressed or also naked, depending on how much time he has paid for. The girl is supposed to 'feel' herself or masturbate in front of the man and he will pay anything from £5 to £20 at the desk for this privilege. For this he will get between ten and forty minutes. In practice the man may ask the girl to do anything, including stand on her head with her tits in her left ear, if he is prepared to pay her more money unofficially once he gets inside the cubicle. Tips range from £10 to £200 for favours which do not usually include darting out of one side and into the other – though this has been known for some that were interviewed.

Prices vary very little and tips vary enormously.

Strip shows

Strip shows vary in type, price etc., according to venue, but also according to what is being provided. Basically there are three categories: grot shows, champagne shows and raunch shows.

Grot shows

These are the pits and can be found in almost every city. The punter enters a rather badly displayed doorway, walks the length of a narrow corridor to a desk, behind which sits a gentleman who generally looks as though he has recently been exhumed. Behind him will be standing one or two rather larger gentlemen, probably retired henchmen from Sicily or Chicago or Brixton. The punter hands money to the zombie, usually between £5 and £10 ($10–$25 in New York) and is then led out of the entrance, because this is only a collection point, and along the road maybe as much as two or three hundred yards to another even grottier venue, down some stairs and along into a back alley, across a courtyard perhaps and into a room, probably no more than twenty feet square with a makeshift stage at the back, a few chairs scattered randomly. A girl suffering from malnutrition, pneumonia and possibly adolescence, will be sitting on the edge of the stage draped in a scarf or sheet. She will probably only execute the minimum amount of movement in order to remove the drape and sit there naked, half asleep. The punter, prior to going into the place, will of course have been asked for a further payment of maybe £10–£20. If he refuses to pay, stating that he has already paid, then he will not be taken in, or rather he will avoid being taken-in. He will not, however, receive a refund of his earlier payment which is presumably a charge for the walk around dingier London or Manhattan. Basically the grot-shows are a complete rip-off.

Champagne shows
Here are the more elaborate versions of the grot-shows where someone, probably aided by a protection racket, has set up a high-class piece of decor with waitresses (usually topless and maybe even bottom-less), tables, lighting, a proper stage and real costume acts. The girls are real strippers and the place has an alcohol licence and maybe food too, though generally only sandwiches. The entrance fee is light, no more than £10 or $20 at the door maximum because the money in these clubs is made from the champagne which ranges in price from £50 ($100) a bottle upwards and is not your best vintage bubbly. Guests

are encouraged, indeed mandated, to drink or leave. The girls receive a commission on the champagne they serve and so will press guests by one means or another into buying as much as they can fit on their small table. Getting through £500 or $1000 in a night is like falling off a log in such establishments, though sometimes the shows can be good, the strippers attractive and the atmosphere entertaining. The waitresses or hostesses are also sometimes available for overtime!

Raunch shows

The third category of strip show can be found in several different forms; in British public houses, in peep-show basements and in private clubs, they are guaranteed to be sexy as hell and generally cost very little, but may be harder to find. In recent years public houses in various parts of England have taken to having a stripper perform while the fellas are drinking at the bar. Some of the shows are extremely good and cost nothing except the price of a beer and tips – optional – to the girls.

In some of the capital city peep shows there are small strip shows on the side which take place either with pornographic movies or as additional entertainment while the punter is waiting for the peep-show girls to change shifts! The stripper will be thrown tips and the entrance charge will be about £3–£5 or $5–$10.

The private clubs are the hardest to find and the most liberal in their style. The shows they put on range from straightforward strip to live sex-shows where the audience is often encouraged to participate.

The club membership will cost around £50–£100 and each visit will cost perhaps £5 plus cost of drinks.

The members are expected to tip the girls, especially if they participate in the live sex-show!

Live sex-shows are more common in countries like the United States, Holland, Denmark and Japan. In Japan a couple can make a substantial living performing in such shows – making in the range of £200 per performance, though the performances go on, taken in turns with perhaps two other couples, for most of the night. People are encouraged to work as couples and not to come hoping to pair off with another. The pay is in cash and the Japanese prefer to see shows with Western performers.

Hostess clubs

Almost every large country in the world has some form of hostess club, scattered in large variety within the city centres. In London the clubs are run on posh lines with discrete and gentlemanly facades. Club membership can be very costly, the drinks are expensive and so are the girls. Membership is in the range of £400 per annum, champagne costs at least £50 per bottle and the girls are available for 'cuddles' and talk in discrete little side seats, hidden enough for foreplay! Most of the girls will be available for sex outside the club and will charge whatever seems suitable. They receive a commission on the drink sold of about 10 per cent of the cover price.

An evening, plus, in a hostess club would set the average punter back around £200 and that might include a belly full of alcohol and a cooperative girl!

Pornography

Pornographic material comes in many forms, but basically in this context consists of magazines and video movies for home and cinema consumption which contain explicit sexual activity between various combinations of male and female (and animal) participants. Magazine material varies so much in cost that there is little point in listing anything. Cinematic or video material available through 'take-out' stores is pretty standard and so also is the price of entrance to porno-cinemas.

Video tapes – purchase-rent

In most of the pornographic shops in New York's Manhattan and London's Soho, together with most of the other major capitals in the world, there is operated a system of 'swop-purchase' for video movies of an explicit pornographic nature. The punter buys a tape for around £30–£40, keeps it for as long as he wishes and then returns the tape for another tape for which he pays half the price again, on each swop. The tapes are generally copies from originals and the quality varies.

Porno-cinemas

The same cities are full of cinema clubs which operate on the basis of a membership fee to cover the law, where necessary, and then an entrance charge. The membership fee will be around £2 in London and the entrance fee anything from a further £2 to £4. The show is continuous through the day from about 11 a.m. to midnight or later and there is no further cost. Most of the peep-show parlours and strip shows and porno book shops also have private cubicles for viewing video-porn by slot machine. In London the slot machines take 50-pence pieces for around five minutes of viewing and in Manhattan the cost is 50 cents for around two minutes. These cubicles are arranged in shops in most other European and Far East cities.

Photo-sessions

The word photo is somewhat of a metaphor in this case as the purpose of the sessions is for punters to get behind a camera in front of which are naked or semi-naked girls writhing or twisting in a state of simulated sexual pleasure! In most major cities there are photo-clubs who supply models for sessions by amateur(?) photographers who are also supplied with a lit studio for one-hour sessions. The clubs also supply processing facilities and charge accordingly.

The one-hour studio sessions cost (typical example in London):

Glamour	solo £15.00	duo £30.00
Continental	solo £18.00	duo £36.00
Advance continental	solo £22.00	duo £44.00
Lesbian		duo £70.00

Stock photos of girls in various poses cost between £5 and £8. Sessions can also be arranged in the punter's home for similar prices plus cab fares.

facts relating to sex and money

1. In Amsterdam the Dutch have got it very well organized, like most other things in Holland. At the Yab Yum men's club you can become a member for about £75 per annum and take advantage of the full facilities of the establishment. At a rate of around

£100 per hour a beautiful girl will be available to you in a sumptuous room with huge double bed (round) and jacuzzi, no restrictions. The Yab Yum club is said to be the most luxurious brothel in the world.

2. The highest circulation 'men's' magazine used to be *Playboy*. In the late 70s Hugh Hefner's empire was overtaken somewhat (at least in the periodical sector) by *Penthouse*, which now sells somewhere in the region of six million copies per month. At a world average £2 retail price that's approximately £140 million revenue per annum. Producing the magazine probably costs around half that figure if you take into account the additional advertising income. Sex pays.

3. Another of the flourishing products produced on the sex market is sold through mail order. Advertised in many of the back pages of the men's magazines are certain 'used garments' which can be purchased from aptly named donors such as 'Kitten' or 'Randy'. They retail in the region of £2 to £5 per pair and according to reports bring a reasonable income for the advertisers.

The same product sold by men does not appear to have similar appeal.

4. The sex software market is flourishing and at many of the world's sex shops it is possible to buy almost any device, ranging from grotesque dildos to various creams for increasing the dimensions of this and that. According to a brief survey the biggest manufacturers of such instruments receive an annual revenue of £12 million. According to their reports the greater the restrictions on the public availability of pornography through the cinemas and videos, the higher their sales.

5. The purchase or hire of pornographic video tapes varies greatly around the world. In New York it is possible to buy an X-rated movie, that is an uncensored movie, on tape, for around £100 if you seek satisfaction on Fifth Avenue. In the seedier parlours of 42nd Street, the same tape will set you back less than £50. In London, presuming that you know where to look, an uncensored porno-movie will cost you about £30 to buy or rent. In Manila the price comes down to about £10 but then so does the quality. In parts of Hong Kong a 'quickie' tape can be rented for a pound.

6. In a survey of all the most popular men's magazines, excluding *Playboy* and *Penthouse*, total circulation amounts to around 22 million copies per month in the US, UK, Australia, Canada and Europe. Purveyors of his type of periodical assess that on average the male buying public buys some four to six of these magazines per month.

Section Eleven

DAILY BREAD

The Latin word for money is *pecunia*, a word derived from the word for a flock of sheep or herd of cattle. Money meant food and sustenance. If nobody had ever thought of making metal disks to exchange for goods, we'd still be trotting about the high streets dragging herds of cattle and flocks of sheep behind us into the various shops and markets. Video rental for one day might cost an arm and a leg!

The 'what it costs to live' list

In the US consumption is popular – everybody makes money to spend it – so it seems sense to find out what they spend it on. Here is a list of the way people spend money, how much they spend and what they spend it on in the US.

1. In 1979 the sum total expenditure of all Americans on all purchases as individuals or householders was $1,510,898,000,000 – that's one trillion, five hundred and ten billion, eight hundred and ninety-eight million dollars – in one year.

2. Out of every $10,000 of income individuals spent:

Food, drink and tobacco which they consumed at home or in restaurants, bars etc:	$2193 (£1370)
Clothes:	$917 (£573)
Housing (rent or mortgage), furniture, utilities, telephone etc., etc.:	$2912 (£1820)
Doctors etc.:	$956 (£597)
Transport:	$1573 (£983)
Education:	$684 (£427)
Recreation:	$784 (£490)

3. The Department of Agriculture in the US estimates that to raise a child born in 1979 to the age of eighteen years will cost $134,414. The first-year costs in 1979 would have been $2972. At the age of six the

annual cost will have risen to $5060; at twelve $9378; and at seventeen $15,624. This assumes an inflation rate of 8 per cent per annum. Over the eighteen-year span food will have cost $32,915 eaten at home and $3730 outside home; clothing $12,129, housing the child $41,121, medical care $6703, transport $20,355 and extra expenses $17,461.

4. In 1979 the Federal Highway Administration worked out that if a US driver purchased a car for $6650 in 1979 it would cost him, to run the car 100,000 miles over the next ten years, a total of $21,717 – or 21.7 cents per mile.

5. Here is a list of the rise in cost of a newly built home in the US with an actual price level and a constant on the value of the dollar, from 1967 to 1980.

	Cost of house	Constant
1964	$20,500	$22,600
1966	$23,300	$24,000
1968	$26,600	$25,500
1970	$26,600	$22,900
1972	$30,500	$24,300
1974	$38,900	$26,300
1976	$48,000	$28,200
1978	$62,500	$32,000
1980	$76,300	$30,900

Bread costs bread

1. More bread for less bread

Money buys less food (and less everything else) as time moves on. Here is a list of typical shopping and the changes in price over ten years in the US.

	1970	1980	% increase
1 lb of coffee	$0.91	$2.82	209
1 lb margarine	$0.30	$0.73	143
1 lb bacon	$0.95	$1.71	80
1 lb butter	$0.87	$1.97	126
1 lb chicken	$0.41	$0.76	85
1 lb onions	$0.16	$0.30	87
1 lb potatoes	$0.09	$0.22	144
1 lb rump steak	$0.73	$1.87	156
1 lb sirloin	$1.35	$2.93	117
1 doz. large eggs	$0.61	$1.00	64

Here is the same list for the UK:

	1970	1980	% increase
1 lb coffee	£0.35	£1.20	342
1 lb margarine	£0.16	£0.42	262
1 lb bacon	£0.38	£1.00	263
1 lb butter	£0.38	£0.60	157
1 lb chicken	£0.25	£0.47	188
1 lb onions	£0.09	£0.17	188
1 lb potatoes	£0.04	£0.11	275
1 lb rump steak	£0.42	£1.10	261
1 lb sirloin	£0.76	£1.95	256
1 doz. large eggs	£0.32	£1.08	337

2. The five most expensive foods in the world:

Truffles	$175 per pound
Beluga caviar	$270 per pound
Dried morel mushrooms	$100 per pound
Foie gras	$75 per pound
Saffron	$55 per pound

3. The annual turnovers for ten top quick-food merchants in the US:

McDonald's Hamburgers	$2,730,000,000
Col. Sanders Kentucky Fried Chicken	$1,165,000,000
Burger King	$ 741,600,000
International Dairy Queen	$ 684,000,000
Pizza Hut	$ 374,200,000
Howard Johnson	$ 358,000,000
Sambo's	$ 348,000,000
Hardee's	$ 324,300,000
Jack-in-the-Box	$ 323,400,000
Burger Chef	$ 305,000,000

Section Twelve

HEAD BREAD

Money is not always a matter of one, two, three; straightforward and simple. Like everything else where numbers are involved it can get confusing simply because of the way it is expressed. Feed an equation through a computer and you'll probably get a straight answer but put 'bread' through the head and results can be very different.

Money puzzles

Brain teasers, anomalies, financial impossibilities –
see if you can work them out. Answers on pp. 226-30.

Money puzzles

The first puzzle
On the Island of Imperfections there are three tribes:
the Pukkas who always tell the truth, the Wotta-
Woppas who never tell the truth, and the Shilli-
Shallas who sometimes tell the truth and sometimes
lie, alternately.

Three inhabitants, Ugly, Stupid and Toothless
(their names should give you some idea of their
characters) take part in our puzzle. The money on
the island is called Hope and the weekly wage of the
Pukka is between 10 and 19 Hopes, the wage of a
Shilli-Shalla is 20 to 29 Hopes and a Wotta-Woppa
gets between 30 and 39 Hopes. They make three
statements each and you don't know which of them
is making the statements:

1 says (a) B is a Wotta-Woppa
      (b) My wages are 25 per cent less than 20
         per cent more than one of the others.
      (c) I get 10 Hopes more than B.

2 says (a) The wage of one of us is different from the sum of those of the other two.
   (b) We all belong to the same tribe.
   (c) More of 3's statements are true than mine.

3 says (a) Ugly earns more than Toothless.
   (b) The wage of one of us is 15 per cent less than the wage of another.
   (c) Stupid is a Shilli-Shalla.

Question: What is 3's name, tribe and wage?

The second puzzle
The Lotaseetas have a rather casual attitude to commerce. Every Monday morning Ming, the rice planter, gathers from the grove outside his bungalow a number of mangoes of uniform weight. For the rest of the week he uses these as weights for measuring out the rice on his scales, charging each customer according to the number of mangoes required to balance the weight purchased.

Unfortunately, the mangoes themselves lose a fixed percentage of their weight each day by evaporation. However, Ming roughly compensates for this by using two mangoes as the unit on Wednesdays and Thursdays and three on Fridays. Clearly, Wednesday is a good day for buying rice and Tuesday is a bad day.

His first customer at precisely 10 o'clock each morning is Fung, the rice merchant, who always buys the same amount of rice for his shop. On Monday Fung's rice cost him 243 cowries. On Friday it cost him 256 cowries.

Question: How much did it cost him on Tuesday?

224

The third puzzle

No organization can be efficient without rules which set out the rewards and responsibilities of the members of the organization. The following are the rules which were put on the notice board of a factory many years ago when the pound was worth a pound and rules were made to be obeyed.

At that time there were five employees in the factory: Alf (A); Bert (B); Charlie (C); Duggie (D); and Ernie (E). Their jobs, not in any order, were door-opener, door-shutter, doorknob-polisher, bottle-washer and welfare officer. The rules read as follows:

(1). Charlie is to get 10 per cent more than the worst paid of you all.

(2). Alf is to be paid more than Duggie.

(3). The bottle-washer is to get 5 per cent more than 10 per cent less than Bert.

(4). Duggie is to get either £1 more or £1 less than Ernie.

(5). The door-opener's wages are to be an odd multiple of 10p.

(6). Ernie is to get 20 per cent more than £1 less than the doorknob-polisher.

(7). The door-shutter is to be the best paid of you all.

(8). Your wages are all to be different and each one is to be a multiple of 10p.

(9). No one is to get more than £20 or less than £10 per week.

Question: What are all their weekly wages?

The fourth puzzle

My three nieces, Anne, Betty and Carole, came to stay with me just before Christmas. When they arrived they handed over their present money and as I wrote down the amounts, in pence, I noticed that they were three-digit numbers using all nine digits (not including zero) and that Anne had more than Betty, and Carole has as much as the other two put together.

I drove the girls into town to shop and as they entered the car to return home they again asked me to look after their money. As I wrote down the three amounts I noticed that they still had amounts in three-digit numbers using all nine digits. Before I drove off they wanted to know how much each had spent. As I told them I was struck by the fact that the answers were still three-digit numbers using all nine digits. I also added that Carole had spent exactly three-fifths of her money while Anne had spent a little more than three fifths of hers.

Question: How much did each girl have for the rest of her stay?

Answers to money puzzles

The first puzzle

The answer is Toothless, Pukka and 17 Hopes.

How come: Consider 1(c) – if this is true then 1 must be a Wotta-Woppa or Shilli-Shalla. But not Wotta-Woppa, for we are assuming that 1(c) is true: therefore 1 would be a Shilli-Shalla and 2 would be

226

Pukka. Therefore 2(c) would be true, but this is not possible. Therefore our assumption is false, therefore 1(c) is not true.

Therefore 1(a) is not true; therefore 2 is not a Wotta-Woppa. If 2 is a Pukka, then 2(c) would be true, but this is not possible, therefore 2 is a Shilli-Shalla! Got it so far? Consider 1(b). If true then 1's wages = $75/100 \times 120/100$ (of 2's or 3's wages) = $9/10 \times$ (2's or 3's).

So 1's wage is 18 Hopes, 27 Hopes or 36 Hopes. Hence either 1(b) is true, 1 is Shilli-Shalla (with 27 Hopes) and 2 or 3 (with 30 hopes) is Wotta-Woppa: or 1(a) is false and 1 is Wotta-Woppa. In either case not all three are Shilli-Shalla.

So 2(b) is false, 2(c) is true, 3 is Pukka and by the above formulation 1 is Wotta-Woppa.

From 3(b) (true) 2 of the wages are in the ratio of $85/100$ i.e. $17/20$.

No one gets a wage of more than 39, therefore the wage of one must be 17 Hopes and of another 20 Hopes. And it must be 3 (Shilli-Shalla) who gets 20 hopes and 3 (Pukka) who gets 17 hopes.

From 3(c), Stupid is Shilli-Shalla, therefore Stupid is 2.

From 3(a), Ugly must be 1 and Toothless must be 3.

The second puzzle
The answer is 324 cowries.

Like this: Let the weight of one mango on Monday be W units, on Tuesday Wx, on Wednesday Wx2, on Thursday Wx3 and on Friday Wx4. Then the cost of the quantity R of rice is:

Monday: R/W currency units (243)
Tuesday: R/Wx currency units
Wednesday: R/2Wx2 currency units
Thursday: R/2Wx3 currency units
Friday: R/3Wx4 currency units (256)

Therefore Monday/Friday = 3x4 = 243/256 and x4 = 81/256.
Therefore x = 3/4 and Tuesday's cost is given by
Tuesday's cost = Monday's cost/x = $243/^3/_4$ = 324.

The third puzzle

Alf is the bottle-washer and he earns £18.90
Bert is the door-shutter and earns £20.00
Charlie is the door-opener and earns £12.10
Duggie is the knob-polisher and earns £11.00
Ernie is the welfare officer and earns £12.00

Work in units of 10p with all wages between 100 and 200 inclusive.

From (3) bottle-washer gets 105/100 × 90/100 × B = 189/200 × B. So bottle-washer earns 189 and B 200. Also B is the best paid and so is the door-shutter.

From (6) E gets more than doorknob-polisher. Hence E is not worst paid, E is 6/5 × (doorknob-polisher − 10) and, being a multiple of 6, is not bottle-washer.

From (1), C's wage is 11/10 × worst wage, which cannot be 189. Also, the worst wage must be a multiple of 10. So C is not bottle-washer: neither is C the worst paid, nor by (2) is A. So D is the worst paid.

From (5) door-opener cannot be D (a multiple of 10), nor E (a multiple of 6). So door-opener is C and, by elimination, D is doorknob-polisher and E is welfare officer.

E's wage is $6/5 \times$ (D's $-$ 10), which is a multiple of 12.

The possibilities are:

D	100	110	120	130	140	150	160	170
C	110	121	132	143	154	165	176	187
E	108	120	132	144	156	168	180	192

But from (4) D gets £1 more or £1 less than E. So D must get 110, E gets 120 and C gets 121.

Q.E.D.

The fourth puzzle
Anne £2.45; Betty £1.69; Carole £3.78

As follows:

Anne   initially has A   spends A1   has left A2
Betty   initially has B   spends B1   has left B2
Carole initially has C   spends C1   has left C2.

where (A, B, C), (A1, B1, C1), (A2, B2, C2) are groups of three digit numbers containing the nine positive digits. Further $C = A + B$, $A = A1 + A2$, $B = B1 + B2$, $C = C1 + C2$.

A is greater than B, $C1 = 3C/5$, A1 slightly greater than $3A/5$. It is known that C is a multiple of 9, it is also a multiple of 5; thus C is an odd number multiple of 45. But C must certainly exceed 50 and contain distinct digits. Hence $C = 675, 765$ or 945. But $C2 = 2C/5 = 270, 306$ or 378. Hence $C2 = 378$, $C = 945$, $C1 = 567$.

Since A is greater than B is greater than 200 there are four solutions of $C = A + B$:

$945 = 628 + 317 = 627 + 318 = 618 + 327 = 617 + 328$.

We now take each of these four solutions in turn and attempt to complete the matrix above with all conditions satisfied. The reasoning is straightforward!

A   628 382 246/ 627 382 245/ 618 3— 2—/
617 3— 2—

B   317 1— 1—/ 318 149 169/ 327 1— 1—/
328 1— 1—

C   945 567 378/ 945 567 378/ 945 567 378/
945 567 378.

There remains then just one solution.

On the following pages are details of Arrow books that will be of interest.

A LITTLE ZIT ON THE SIDE

Jasper Carrott

He's been a delivery boy (the terror of Solihull), a toothpaste salesman (for four hours), a folkie (repertoire – two songs) – and the most unlikely and original comic superstar for years.

Now Jasper Carrott reveals more of the outrageous talent that has taken him from the Boggery to a series of one-man shows that won him ITV's Personality of the Year Award.

Discover the do-it-yourself man, how to become star of Top of the Pops and the Carrott guide to dog-training. Relive the simple pleasures of The Magic Roundabout, Funky Moped and the Mole.

THE GREAT ESCAPE

Paul Brickhill

There could be no other war book like *The Great Escape*, Paul Brickhill's celebrated, classic account of the heroic and tragic breakout from Stalag Luft III.

'The high-water mark of all active prisoner-of-war books . . . I found myself putting it down almost literally to get my breath. Scattered through its packed and racing pages are a hundred tiny incidents and characters worthy of mention, indelibly etched on a reader's memory' *Daily Telegraph*

'One of the most unputdownable stories of the war' *The Observer*

'A tale of group heroism, determination and ingenuity which gets hold of the reader's nerves and emotions and won't let go' *Sunday Times*

THE UNSAFE SKY

William Norris

Southern England: An approaching aircraft 'filled the wind-shield' of a passenger airliner . . .

Newfoundland: A jumbo jet goes into a dive as all four engines die . . .

Washington: A landing DC9 misses the tail fin of a departing DC10 by twenty feet . . .

Only luck prevents mistakes like these from becoming tragedies on the scale of Zagreb, Tenerife and Chicago – and yet many similar incidents are never even reported.

Why do they happen? Can they be prevented? Can they be controlled? This terrifying investigation reveals not only the potential dangers of human error, but how commercial pressure, inadequate or ignored safety procedures, out-dated equipment, confusion in the cockpit and obsessive secrecy all combine to make air travel increasingly perilous.

Those who provided information for this book have done so from their concern that air travel may be approaching a crisis in safety. The evidence gathered by William Norris confirms such fears.

GULLIBLE'S TRAVELS

Billy Connolly

He has travelled from the majestic deserts of Doha (twin town of Drumchapel in Scotland) and the teeming markets of Bletchley to the splendour of the Sydney surf and the exotic decadence of the Crawley Leisure Centre.

And here it is — a unique guide to the world, travel, life, death and camel-smells, as seen through the eyes of

'the gangling Glaswegian doyen of bad taste' *Daily Telegraph*

'the man who makes Bette Midler look like Jess Conrad' *The Stage*

'one of the most outrageous Scotsmen ever to have vaulted Hadrian's Wall' *Daily Express*

'the laughing laureate of the loo' *The Times*

the inimitable (thank God) BILLY CONNOLLY

Compiled by Duncan Campbell

Illustrated by Steve Bell

THE TESTAMENT OF ANDROS

James Blish

A disaster-investigator of the future, whose craft is the reading of dead men's minds . . .

A polluted, dying Earth where power is in the hands of the almighty International Brotherhood of Sanitary Engineers . . .

Minute aquatic human colonists, genetically bred to settle an underwater world . . .

A woman space pioneer who unwittingly brings hetero-sexuality to the primeval life of Titan . . .

All this – and more: the best of the best from one of the true giants of modern SF.